Conduit:
[A Collection of Poems and S[...]
Jon Goode]

D0153469

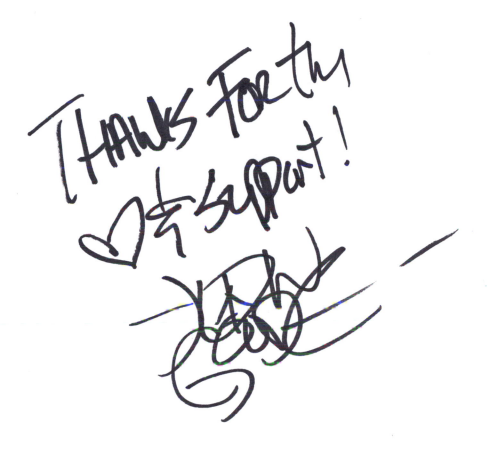

Thanks For thy ♡ & Support!

Conduit:

[A Collection of Poems and Short Stories by

Jon Goode]

GOODESTUFF ENT LLC

Atlanta, GA

Copyright ©2015 by Jonathan Goode

All rights reserved. This book or any portion thereof may not be reproduced, republished or used in any manner whatsoever without the express written permission of the publisher except for the use of brief excerpts in book, magazine, newspaper or electronic publication reviews. For permission requests, write to the publisher, addressed "Attention: Permissions Coordinator," at the email address below:
Jon.goode.writer@gmail.com
Printed in the United States of America
First Printing, 2015

ISBN-13:
978-0996500487
ISBN-10:
0996500480

GOODESTUFF ENT LLC
Cover photo by: Steve Eberhardt
Cover photo taken at ebrik's coffee room, Atlanta Ga.
Editor: Dr. Lia Bascomb

Dedicated

To John E. Goode Jr., Barbara Goode and Tiffany Goode. Thank you for believing in me before I believed in myself.

TABLE OF CONTENTS:

CHAPTER SIX

CHAPTER SEVEN

PREFACE
By
Jon Goode

With great frequency I've discussed with other writers my feelings surrounding the idea that I don't actually write my poems. That is not to say that I plagiarize my poems, no not at all. In the ways that people think of poems, plays, short stories or novels as written by an individual my poems are certainly, in those ways, written by me. What I mean when I say that I don't write my poems is that my poems always feel like a gift given to me by my forefathers, by my ancestors and by God. I cannot tell you the number of times I've written a poem then afterward looked at what is on the page only to discover that I have no idea where these words, concepts or ideas have come from. What is on the page is more often than not beyond me and yet a complete extension and expression of the part of me that is connected to you, to we and to us since the beginning of time.

When I've expressed these thoughts to peers and contemporaries I've repeatedly received nods of agreement, warm smiles and soft eyes that silently say, "You get it!" In the ways expressed above I think that many writers think of themselves as middle men, as go betweens, as conduits granted the great honor and gargantuan responsibility of bringing forth from those long gone; necessary and needed ideas, concepts and stories that educate, sometimes entertain and always, in some way, enlighten contemporary audiences.

Amir Sulaiman states it quite eloquently in his poem Cornerstore Folklore when he says,
"… The characteristics that cause you to love me/ they're not really from me/ they come from above me/ similar to sun beams that descend from the heavens to hug me/ and I become like photosynthetic with roots and green leaves/ and the rest just kind of works out lovely/ and

this just came to me recently as an epiphany/ that the artist of my art isn't really me/ and the poems aren't mine they merely visit me/ and it really isn't accurate to thank me but the creator of creativity/ absolutely independent of us and relativity…"

That verse captures the very essence of why I've entitled this collection Conduit. I hope you enjoy.

CHAPTER ONE

"Mother is the name for God in the lips and hearts of little children." - William Makepeace Thackeray

"Back in the day when I was young, I'm not a kid anymore but some days I sit and wish I was a kid again." - Ahmad

"It took me 100 years to turn 18, after that every year felt like a day."- Leonard Starkey

Barbara

Mess up in school by the teacher I'd get beat;
Come home and I'd catch it from Mrs. Taylor across the street.
Then my mom would come along beating my butt on the lawn
Talking about, "Wait 'til your daddy gets home!"
And I'm like for what?
I'm a little cat I ain't got but so much butt
But I swear she was determined that she was going to spank it all.
"Go get me a switch!" came the call.
"Bring two!
Because I know how you and your sister do!"
You see kids will be kids but moms will be moms
And you done did what you did and mom's going to show you right from wrong.
And I'm going to tell y'all something that some folks just don't understand;
She wasn't trying to raise a friend, she was trying to raise a man.
So every now and again she had to raise her hand
But there was love in her means and love in her ends.
But a lot of folks are out here living loveless.
They're trying to raise a child they can go to the club with.
They won't take their child to church but together smoke cess
And if they cared more maybe these kids wouldn't be so careless.
Ya'll have been to the mall and the grocery store.
Ya'll know, these kids really run the show.
I saw this kid curse his mom he couldn't have been no more than four.

2

Had that been me I would have been picking my lil butt up off the floor.

She'd have spanked me right there in the grocery store.

She'd have spanked me right there on aisle four.

She'd have smacked my lil butt on the way out the door.

And I bet I wouldn't mess up in the store any more.

Hell I might not even go to the store any more!

For those that don't know

Let me tell you how it's supposed to go:

You put sir and ma'am after everything you say,

You get out of those school clothes before you go out to play,

You finish your home work before you think about going out,

And before those street lights hit you get your butt back in this house!

"…But, but Billy's mom lets him stay out for an extra few."

"Boy I don't give a d@m what Billy's momma do!"

I will beat you, I will beat Billy… I will beat Billy's momma too!"

That's how my mom used to do

She'd be coming for your issue;

And just before bed on your forehead gently kiss you.

She'd sing a song or two

Or play a game with you

Or spell your name with you

Or teach you two and two.

I'm old school I had that Speak and Spell

You know, "The cow goes moo."

But let me ask you this

What the hell was a Pikachu?

What was a Pokemon, a Ferbie

What the hell was a Teletubbie?

I remember the simple days

When it was Easy Bake Ovens and My Buddy

Barbie and Ken, G.I. Joe and a Schwinn;

Rock Em Sock Em Robots!

We used to play Connect Four!

Pretty sneaky sis,

They don't play games like that any more.

And that's it maybe

Because Playstation has driven them crazy.

House of the Dead, Doom and Resident Evil

Have made them pretty good shots;

And then the internet will lead you

To where the guns get bought.

Now you do the math people and tell me what you've got.

It's like Columbine High, multiple guns shots.

The parents are standing around like, "Well who would have thought?"

And I'm looking at them like, Well YOU should have thought!

And you should have taught and maybe you should have fought.

My mom didn't assume she knew exactly what was in my room;

Underneath the bed and in the dresser drawers.

I was like, "But momma that's mine!"

And she was like, "Ain't nothin' up in here yours!"

She said, "You ain't paying no bills and if you don't stop slamming these doors!"

Build bombs around my moms? I was too busy doing chores.

But I loved my childhood I don't know about yours.

For me it was ice cream trucks in the summer,

Candy lady on the corner,

Hide and seek.

Kick ball, dodge ball, trick or treat;

Freeze tag you're it and tell me who could forget;

You and all your friends, "Hey! Put your foot in...

Bubble gum, bubble gum in the dish

How many bubble gum do you wish..."

Where I'm from that was a hit

And you have to admit

That kids these day just don't know what they have missed.

CHAPTER TWO

"God has no religion." — Mahatma Gandhi

My God

My God is colorblind,
Crossed picket and color lines
Stood in the thickets against the wicked
And heard my mother's cries.
He's carried crosses
And picked cotton with my sisters and brothers
I'm talking about, my God.

The same God
That my mom and dad told me to
Fear, respect; and be quiet and be still
When the thunder cracked loud and rain came down hard.

The same God
That when the stats said by the age of eighteen
I'd be dead or behind bars
Covered me in his grace
So that I could face and defy the odds.

The same God
That I pray to on my knees
Spoke to Joseph in his dreams
Parted the red sea
Raised Elijah amongst the stars;
And lately I've been thanking him
For the hard times
Because it's in those times that my lessons come
That my blessings come.

I have a little more than a few
And a lot less than some

But anything I have comes from nothing I've done.
I'm still living off the prayers from my great grandma's tongue.
I'm still blessed by the hymns that my late grandma sung
To honor the holy spirit, the heavenly father and the son.
Oh, my God.

Mastectomy

She was the definition of beauty.
She was tall,
She was completely bald,
She was fresh out of recovery
From her mastectomy.
Being a breast amputee
Made her no less of a woman to me.
Those lumps of flesh across her chest made breasts
But breasts have never made a woman and breast never made she.
And she?
She held her head high
With a sense of peace in her eyes
That could not be denied
And could not be described or explained if I tried.
Sustained by her sense of faith
And her sense of pride
As she began to walk
You could sense it in her stride.
She stuck her chest out and dared your eyes not to notice
That the disappearing act was a fact and not some hocus pocus.
That's how I came to hear what she said to a man who came near
To offer his condolences.
She said, "I want you to understand and please know this.
Yes,
I've second guessed
God and at times asked why.
And yes,
Alone in the dark
I oft times cry.
But when my eyes are blessed to greet a new day
I understand that I have to live at least two days, today.

And I understand that in someway
This is all in God's plan
So I've laid my burdens down
And taken up God's hand;
Because when the chemo goes long
And I'm not so sure that I can go on
God gives me a shoulder that I can lean and rely on.
And when I don't want no more Ensure
And I'm not so sure I can endure any more
And I fall to the floor;
Not wanting to die but not truly understanding what I'm living for;
Not understanding who I am,
Not understanding what am I to do
That's when God takes me in his arms and he carries me through.
And yes people love comparing me to
The strong and the brave
From Ali to MLK
But what I do is not brave
Because I, just like they
Do what I have to do.
Step in my Dr. Scholls
And you'll see neither my shoes nor my soul
Have walked an easy road
But I remember being told,
It's not the path you choose
But the path that chose you.
The same quandary faced Luke, Mark, John and Mathew.
So I laugh at those who view this as a tragedy
It seems sad you see
But I used to live the life of Sadducees.
So don't be sad for me;
This had to be.
Sometimes the buildings destroyed in catastrophes

Were simply blocking some things you had to see.
And right now let me
Clear up some of the fallacies associated with my malady.
Though the chemo leaves me weak
My soul is so complete
That even when I cannot speak
You can see, feel and hear me through my smile;
And when this earthly host is gone
And my ghost is carried home
I'll live on through a poem
And be reborn as a child floating down the Nile.
Though I may have Cancer
Cancer will never have me!
Bald with one breast
I am more and no less
Than any woman you will ever see.
I am yesterday,
I am tomorrow,
I am now and forever me.
I never asked you to pity or revel in me.
I never asked for your pardon or revelry.
My mind is more concerned
With the current turns taken in society.
You know just the other week I saw The Passion of Christ
On a movie screen.
I saw his pain depicted in some very moving scenes.
But if I can't find the passion of Christ
In everyday human beings
Then 300 mil in tickets sales … what does it all mean?
Understand these infants
These seeds that we've sown will grow
Into little visions of we.
My trials and tribulations

Have shown it's so much bigger than me.
I'm trying to see these acorns grow into bigger and better trees;
And I'd give the other breast
If I thought that would help you to see and believe."
And on that note she turned to me
She gave a smile, she took her leave
And she
Was oh so beautiful.

"One Sunday a man visits a very popular mega-church only to be denied entry due to his attire. He's sitting on the steps of the church feeling dejected when Jesus walks up, sits beside him and says, 'Don't worry, they won't let me in either.'"-[A joke told to me by my father]

Long Dollar

Mr. Jones in his Sunday's best pacing;
Mrs. Jones in her Sunday dress waiting impatient
For the ushers to begin
To usher in the church congregation
To hear about God's salvation
And Satan's temptation.
The flock heavy with sin
The church a weigh station
While pastor lay in wait to waylay 'em,
Lift lions and slay lambs at the gate
Testify, pacify and pass the plate
(Pass the plate).

And the Choir sang their songs
The congregation sang along
Waving their hands
And their Martin Luther King fans
But they weren't fans of Martin Luther
Or Christ the martyr
They worshipped at the altar of the Long Dollar

(Of the Long Dollar)
(Of the Long Dollar).

And there I am eighteen years old
Running in late dressed in street clothes;

12

And when my feet hit the church doors
In jeans and shelltoes
It seemed hell froze.
I was greeted with heaven help's
And hell no's
I suppose those folks in salvation's army
Fo sho don't shop at the Salvation Army.
They all smelled like obsession.
I pray the scent of salvation's on me.

And the Choir sang their song
The congregation sang along
Waving their hands
And their Martin Luther King fans
But they weren't fans of Martin Luther
Or Christ the martyr
They worshipped at the altar of the Long Dollar
(Of the Long Dollar)
(Of the Long Dollar).

The preacher screamed, "No weapon formed can harm me!"
Which seemed right he had a right tight army.
In fact I bet not a single congregant had even touched the hem of his
garment yet.
So I sat in the front row right next to Ms. So & So
She wore her skirt real high and her hat real low.
You know, that it was known to everyone
That after the pastor would make her speak in tongues.
No one was sure if he was reaching them
But the shepherd sheared the sheep
He was surely fleecing them.
He was preaching and teaching to the young
Telling them who they are and who they should become;

And behind doors he was touching them
Right under parents' nose he was touching them
Soon it was exposed that he was touching them
(He was touching them)
(He was touching).

And the Choir sang their songs
The congregation sang along
Waving their hands
And their Martin Luther King fans
But they weren't fans of Martin Luther
Or Christ the martyr
They worshipped at the altar of the Long Dollar
(Of the Long Dollar)
(Of the Long Dollar).

"Don't let anybody take your manhood. Be proud of our heritage; as somebody said earlier tonight, we don't have anything to be ashamed of. Somebody told a lie one day. They couched it in language. They made everything black, ugly and evil. Look in your dictionary and see the synonyms of the word "black." It's always something degrading and low and sinister. Look at the word, "white." It's always some pure, high and clean. Well I want to get the language right tonight. I want to get the language so right that everybody here will cry out, "Yes I'm Black! I'm proud of it! I'm Black and beautiful!"-Dr Martin Luther King Jr.

Me, My God and My Destiny [A tribute to Martin Luther King Jr.]

I keep having this reoccurring dream
And in this dream I sit alone in a room in Tennessee
And it's just me,
My God
And my destiny.
And I feel like I've given this world the best of me
But now I can hear the balcony
And the balcony is calling for the rest of me.
And I can hear its sweet song like the Sirens of the Odyssey
And it's got to be
The American Melting pot that unlocked the recipe for this tragedy.
They took warriors, kings and queens
From their homeland and had them told that they were 3/5ths of human beings.
It was America that tried to convince them of this.
Add in gashes from master's fists,
Heavy lashes from the whips
And queens forced to push master's bastards from their hips
While their kings are forced to sit…
Helpless and watch this.

15

It was their masters who tried to convince them that this was right.
Add in a middle passage that lasted longer than most's life.
Dashing through the cotton field seeking freedom in the night.
Death in the cotton field offers the only freedom in the light.
Slowly we begin to see things in a different light.
Slowly we begin to understand that every woman, child and man
Has certain inalienable rights.
Nat Turner and John Brown they laid their life down
When they took up the fight
And no one had to convince them that this was right.
And here I sit in a cold sweat in this room in Tennessee
And it's just me,
My God
And my destiny.
And I am looking to the heavens like if this is thy will then let it be.
I will walk the same road as the shepherds who came ahead of me.
I will carry the same load as the martyrs who died instead of me.
Moses and Harriet Tubman they led woman children and men
Across burning sands and through swamp land
To the freedom promised them.
And I
I have walked from Selma to Montgomery
With a multitude behind me and an angry hoard in front of me
With nothing but the strength of the Lord up under me
And the weight of the world on my shoulders.
But I will not back peddle and I will not retreat.
I will not concede defeat.
I've seen the fate of those who've come before me.
I've looked into the face of Hoover and those who abhor me.
I've been arrested in Georgia.
I'm detested in Tennessee, Alabama and Mississippi
But if God be for me
Who can stand against me?

He has blessed me and let me
Stand on Lincoln's steps in the heart of DC
And deliver a speech so passionate and unique
About my dreams for Equality
That it reached my detractors and made them acknowledge me.
It was filled with so much truth some of them began to follow me.
I tell you I have moved mountains with mere mustard seeds.
And all that's left for me
Is what awaits on this balcony.
I stand face to face with my destiny
And the irony
Is that no man really lives that long;
But through my death maybe my dream could live on;
Through those of you who find the voice to sing freedom's song;
Through those of you who speak of our struggles to your daughters and
your sons;
Through those of you who pick up the baton and continue to race on;
Through those of you who understand that freedom is for all
Or freedom is for none.
Our fight is for the all
And our fight is for the one
Until God's will for us all be done.
I tell you I had a dream
That I was alone in Tennessee
And it was just me,
My God
And my Destiny.

Proverbs 24:16 "For a just man falleth seven times, and riseth up again…"

8

Laying on my back staring at the sun…

I'd begun to think about the first time I'd ever been knocked down to the ground.
It happened back when I used to stay 'round the corner from the neighborhood playground
And I can't even say now what that fight was even about.
This kid hit me in the nose.
I fell down, I rose, I hit that kid in the mouth;
And that's just about where it all begins and ends.
We didn't hold any punches but didn't hold any grudges
And thirty minutes after boxing me and that kid were best friends.
All was forgotten and all was forgiven.
And some say turning the other cheek
Is for wimps, geeks and women
But anyone can give in and strike out with aggression.
We beefed like boys
But we walked away like men
And therein lay a valuable lesson.

I roll up from my back and rest where my elbow bends…

Then my mind continues to spin around
To the second time I can remember being knocked down to the ground.
It was by my dad.
He hit me square in the chest after I had brought home bad grades.
With tears in his eyes he stood perfectly still and stated,

18

"I ain't hit you half as hard as reality will if you grow up black, poor and uneducated."
So I got to my feet and eventually matriculated
To college where in 4, 5 … 6 years I eventually graduated.
It was clear he hadn't wasted
This physical conversation on education and progression.
Some would call it tough love
But love, it's a tough world and therein lay a valuable lesson.

I stop staring at the sun.
I look down at the ground and will myself up to my knees…

The third time had to be when I was roughly fifteen.
I'd just seen the movie Breakin'
And decided I was in love with this girl named Arlene
She was Haitian;
And although she was taken to me it seemed
That she was mine for the taking;
But her boyfriend's fists decided to remind me about touching other people's things
And possessions.
They say trying to tend other people's garden
Is how yours goes rotten
And therein lay a valuable lesson.

The fourth had to be when my parents got divorced.
Well they didn't really get divorced they just kind of decided they weren't married anymore.

The fifth had to be after I'd enlisted in the Marine Corps.
They called me in my college dorm
And said, "We call this Operation Desert Storm
And your black @ss is going to war!"

The sixth had to be when my lady told me

That she'd missed her period;

At a period in my life when I just wasn't ready to hear it.

But eventually I got my head on straight

And couldn't wait for the date

That my baby would awake,

Look at me and smile.

The seventh had to be while

In her second month my lady miscarried the baby

And the doctors had to say to me,

"I'm sorry Mr. Goode… but there will be no child."

And the sky turned dark.

My heart and world turned grey.

I'd been knocked down and out.

I thought I had nothing left to say.

I was down for the count.

I thought I'd never stand on another stage.

But I stand here today to say to you

That life is a fight and you're going to get knocked down a time or two.

It's a fifteen round bout and you're bound to lose a round, or two.

But I'm going to tell you what you do.

Between rounds you have to breathe,

Prepare and pray to get you through.

During rounds, stick and move

Think win, never lose

And therein lay a valuable lesson;

Because just when I thought I was down for the count

Just then I started thinking about all of my life's blessings

And I moved from my knees to my feet.

Because in this fight against life
We're all going to have to stand and greet
Our fears and our fate
Face to face
And when you meet
You look them in the eyes straight
Held up by nothing but your beliefs and your faith.
Because if life knocks you down seven times
You're going to have to stand up

8.

Love Thy Neighbor

He hasn't been touched by another human being in so long;
And he knows Lord
That his past is prologue
But the doctors told him
That his future is not so far off.
So in the present
He just wants someone, anyone, to hold him;
To unwrap and unfold him
To see who he is on the inside and to love him any way.
Many say he's a white elephant gift.
That once the paper is ripped
And the secret concealed
Is revealed, the veil lifted
He's instantly reviled
Rejected and re-gifted.
Because who could love such a thing as this?
Muslims in their mosques
Scoff and throw rocks in the street
The Hadith says you can indeed shoot
Those who have done the indecent deed of Loot;
And Abraham's other kids
Think of the Torah
Of Sodom and Gomorrah.
God's iron fist;
And so in time the New Testament's
Mathew 22:39 will be quickly dismissed
Because who could hug such a thing as this?
And although Christians say
And daily remind that Christ is the way
And that his parables teach
Love, Forgiveness

And To turn the other cheek.
They still will not turn a kind eye.
They walk the church aisle once a week
But won't let that message seep inside
To Love thy neighbor as thy…
Self;
And sometimes your neighbor needs your help;
And sometimes your neighbor doesn't look like you
Or anyone else
That you know.
Sometimes you neighbor wouldn't do the things you do
And you wouldn't go the places your neighbor would go
But lo and behold he is still your neighbor!
And
Sometimes your neighbor is sinking in the sand
And could use a hand from above.
And sometimes your neighbor needs something as simple as a kind
word, a smile and a hug.
Love thy neighbor doesn't mean you have to be who your neighbor is
Or do what your neighbor does.
So when did we become so unforgiving, so uncaring, so devoid of
love?
Did you know
That Westboro Baptist Church
Hands its members signs that say
Death to all who are gay?
And they believe they are doing God's work.
But they ignored God's word that states this,
"When he saw the crowds, he had COMPASSION on them, because
they were HARASSED and HELPLESS, like sheep without a
SHEPHERD," MATTHEW 9:36.
But they ignored that profession
And picketed the funeral of Matthew Shepard;

A college student in Wyoming

That was tied to a fence

Beaten and killed because he was gay

And some say he needed to be taught a lesson;

And so they taught him to death.

And they did the same thing

When they picketed the funeral and final rest of Coretta Scott King;

A woman whose husband fought and died for equal rights

And she continued the fight, she lived and died for the same things.

And to bring picket signs designed

To illicit feelings of fear, anger and pain

To a ceremony that already finds family and friends

Emotions tested

And strained,

Does not ring of the will of my God…

And by God in the present

He just wants someone to hold him

To unwrap and unfold him

To see who he is on the inside and love him any way.

And he understand that when he says,

I am gay and I have HIV

That what people hear him say

Is, I am gay and don't touch me

Or

I am gay and don't trust me

Or

I am gay and don't love me.

But what he is really trying to say is don't push me away.

He's saying I have HIV and I am gay

But could you love and pray for me anyway?

Could YOU love such a thing as this?

Because when asked which

Was the greatest of the commandments

Jesus came to say:
Love thy God with thy heart, soul and mind
But second and in kind
Is love thy neighbor as thy self
And on these two all the other laws rest.
So let your judgments all rest
And for the love of God just
Give him a hug.

"You okay?"

"Yeah … Yeah I'm alright."

"How were things down at the poll? I hear it was a madhouse with all that Yes We Can'ing."

"It was crazy. It was beautiful and it was crazy and it was … huhm… Have I ever told you the story of Arthur Edwin?"

"I'm sorry?"

"Arthur Edwin. Have I ever told you his story? My uncle told it to me when I was a boy. I know your grandmother filled your head with all manner of tales about frogs and princesses, fairies and fantasies; and I was so busy telling the boys what not to do and beating them when they did it anyway that by the time I looked up you were a grown woman on your way to college. I probably never got around to telling it to ya. Hell! I'd forgotten all about it myself until this very day."

"Pop pop! What did I tell you about cursing?"

"You told me not to f##king cuss … so did I tell you or not?"

"No I don't believe that you've ever mentioned…"

"I would like very much to tell you his story today. I would like that very very very much."

"Okay … uhm, let me take my coat off first."

"Okay… tell me when you're ready … you ready?"

"Alright pop alright don't get yourself so worked up, I'm here and I'm ready to hear your story about Ethan Allen."

"Arthur Edwin, it's …"

"That reminds me I need to call about that chair I ordered."

"Never mind, by the end you'll know his name, of that I'm sure. In Alabama in 1925 two things were birthed, do you know what they were?"

"I'm sure I have no idea."

"One was the Wilson Dam which stretched across Lauderdale and Colbert Counties; the second was the legend of Arthur Edwin which

26

has stretched across time itself. I don't know if you know this but a lot of our folk are originally from Alabama. I was one of the first to move to Atlanta. I only mention Alabama because most people think the story of Arthur Edwin begins in Birmingham but really it starts before that in Tupelo, Mississippi or Gum Pond as I heard it called by some due to all the black gum trees. Well in 1860, one year before the Civil War, John Edwin was born on the Edwin plantation in Tupelo. John was born to a slave woman but he come out so white that if you didn't know any better you'd have thought he was the master of the plantation Edward Edwin's baby; and if you'd have known the better of the truth you'd have known he really was Edward Edwin's baby. Now young John was only four years old when General Andrew Smith and the union troops set their sights on Tupelo. In the confusion of the battle between General Smith and General Forest a lot of slaves found their freedom earlier than anticipated, they released themselves on their own recognizance. John Edwin and his mother were two of the many that decided that it was better to die on the run than live on beneath the boot."

"Uhm pop pop…"

"Yeah?"

"Does this pick up? I mean God bless you and the history channel and all, but if Chicken George, Clarence Thomas or Madea make an appearance I'm out."

"What you got better to do? Play with your wee wee?"

"It's not a wee wee, it's a wii? Girls don't even have … please go on. You know what, it was my fault for stopping you."

"D@#n right!"

"Pop pop! The cursing!"

"Listen now, I was just getting to the interesting part. So the Civil War ends in 1865 and John and his mother bounce around quite a bit before finally settling in Anniston Alabama in 1870 by this time John is ten and looks as white as Sean Hannity in a flour mill during a snow storm, so his mother passes herself off as his mammy. The story is circulated

27

around town that John's family was killed in the war and that he and his mammy escaped slaughter at the hands of the Yankees by the skin of their teeth and the point of a bayonet. That story makes John somewhat of a local celebrity, a boy his age that had the guts to stand up to those damned Yankees! The story so impressed Robert Kendrick, a local landowner that he allowed John to work and apprentice on his plantation. Well long story not so long John learns under Kendrick's tutelage how to run a farm and work the land. In time he makes enough money to secure his own tract of land near Birmingham Alabama. John ends up taking on a bunch of sharecroppers to work the land. No one knows he's not white of course but what they do know is that he pays them a decent wage and treats them fairer than they've ever been treated. This earns him the title of nigger lover to the rest of the local white folk. Ironically the title nigger lover also makes him one of the most popular men to be in the employ of in the entire state of Alabama because if you are a so-called nigger who better to work for than someone that they say loves you? In time he falls for a daughter of one of the sharecroppers in his employ. He tells everyone that she's being hired on as his maid and sets her up with a small private residence that connects to the main house. They live secretly as husband and wife. In 1903 she gives birth to their one and only child, a boy that they named Arthur, Arthur Edwin."

"That was wonderful pop pop, alright then…"

"That's not the story of Arthur Edwin. That's just a little bit of background I'm just getting to the story."

"Are you serious?"

"Yes I'm serious, that was just the cornbread! I'm about to give you the meal now."

"Well thank you for the cornbread, I'm full. You can have the collards and chittlins and whatever else all to yourself. I'm out."

"Seriously what else do you have to do? You act like you've got a fire lit in your panty draws. Where else do you have to be? Is it with that boy with the square head that lives down the street? He is stretching the devil out of those sweaters trying to get 'em over that noggin of his."

"Go on pop pop…"

"I'm serious he is the poster child for C sections."

"Pop pop! Go on now."

"Alright then stop interrupting me d@mmit! Where was I!?

"1903!"

"Oh yes! 1903. So, Arthur's complexion favored his mother and no one knew that John Edwin was his father. Many of the kids born in that time were given the name of the plantation or landowner that the people worked for. The plantation's master was sort of viewed as the almighty father of them all so who better to name your child after? But unlike many black folks in the south at that time John made sure that Arthur was well educated. Arthur was after all his one and only son and he loved him like any father would, even if he couldn't openly show or publicly express that love."

"That's sad."

"Sad indeed. Well in the fall of 1924 at the age of twenty one with a recently read copy of the fifteenth amendment to the constitution in his hand, and no real sense of the racial intolerance of Birmingham Alabama in his heart, Arthur Edwin got the notion in his head that he was fittin' to vote. Now mind you we're talking about 1924 in Birmingham; not Birmingham, England but Birmingham, Alabama! You have to understand that in 1924 in Birmingham, Alabama everything black was despised, hell they'd have lynched the night if they coulda caught it. But Arthur had read that the fifteenth amendment guaranteed him the unmitigated right to stand shoulder to shoulder with white men and vote. His father and mother caught wind of his inkling and expressly forbade him to do anything so foolish as to go down to the courthouse amongst some of the angriest white men the south had ever produced and try to vote. But Arthur's mind was made up. Arthur had heard about the poll tax being levied by some of the more vigilant members of the white citizenry so he took three dollars from his father's bureau. He was not a thief you understand but nothing and no one was going to bar him from casting his ballot. He was going to vote for Calvin Coolidge even if it killed him, one because it was his right to vote and two because the slogan "Keep Cool with Coolidge," spoke to him on some strange level, Teapot Dome be damned.

The National Guard had been deployed to ensure that all those that wanted to vote and had the poll tax to pay would be allowed to vote with no incident. This didn't sit well with Governor Thomas Erby Kilby, Sr. but it was the President's call, not his. You're probably wondering if I'm speaking of the same Governor Thomas Erby Kilby, Sr. that had an Alabama centennial half dollar minted in his honor while he was living, and a prison erected in his name, that still stands today, after his death."

"I was wondering no such thing."

"Yes ma'am, that was him, one and the same. So Arthur walked up to the polling station amidst the National Guard's troops and made his way through the phalanx of white faces that had nothing good or encouraging to say to him. He was undaunted. It was his intention to stand as a man and cast his vote.

Arthur made his way to the door and informed the poll tax assessor that he was there to vote. He was told it would cost him fifty cent, when he produced the fifty cent he was told it would cost a dollar, when he produced the dollar he was told it would cost him two and when he produced the two he was told it would cost him his life. Unfettered Arthur walked in, filled out his ballot and slipped it into the ballot box. Arthur had voted, he'd done something that no one in his family had ever done before, he'd exercised his constitutional right, he'd stood up to the racists, stood up to his own fear and stood up for his people. Later that night in the Birmingham woods he stood up on his tiptoes, his hands tied behind his back as they slipped the noose around his neck and pulled it taut. Their breath smelled of corn liquor and hatred; their eyes were blood shot and filled with blood lust. He had no illusions; he knew that this was going to be his last night on earth; that

30

tomorrow was going to be as the hymn says, that great getting up morning where you go to see your savior. He felt his feet leave the ground and could hear the rope grating against the limb of the tree with the lynch mob's every pull on it. The men cheered as he began to flail. They shouted at no one in particular, they shouted at each other, they shouted at the black night to let that be a lesson to anyone trying to change things in Alabama. Amidst their raucous celebration and grandiose declarations Arthur Edwin's body stopped flailing, his eyes rolled back into his head and he became deathly still. The mob was so lost in celebration, no one even noticed.

John Edwin had caught wind of what Arthur had done and had set out to find him when he came across the mob singing and dancing while the body of his son hung overhead. He'd arrived just as Arthur had stopped moving. The sight of nigger loving John Edwin in their midst had a somewhat sobering effect on the mob. They asked John if he had finally seen the light and come to join them on their divine campaign to preserve Alabama. Fighting the sorrow in his heart and the paternal rage boiling in his belly John Edwin calmly told them no he had not, but that boy hanging from that tree was in his employ and he wanted him cut down so that he could give him a proper funeral and burial. Now that didn't sit very well with many in the group. The phrase nigger lover began to rise up in their throats. John could see the lack of rationale and murderous fervor that the lynching had done nothing but exacerbate in their minds and hearts. The men began to slowly approach him pointing their fingers and informing him that either he was with them or against them. John's fight or flight response kicked in. He was well into his sixties and knew he couldn't take on all these men, so he did what so many had done before him, he took off running into the night. The mob gave chase but after consuming so much moonshine I don't think you could actually call their feeble and failed attempts to catch John Edwin a chase. After pursuing him for a minute, losing sight of him and shouting some profanities in the general direction of his retreat they headed back to the scene of the crime where

31

their intent was to cut down Arthur's body, hack off his fingers and ears as souvenirs, drag the body into town and have it propped up for display in front of the local barber shop as a warning to any other of the local niggers with thoughts of getting out of line. The only problem was that upon their return, the body was gone. The noose was just swinging slack and empty in the wind.

The mob's immediate thought was that somewhere in all of the running around John Edwin had doubled back and taken Arthur down off that noose. They resigned themselves to dealing with him come morning. The next morning found fifteen men standing on the steps of John Edwin's house. Where's the body they demanded. They apologized to John for chasing after him and threatening his life. He was still considered a white man after all and that kind of behavior was just flat out rude. They told him that it was born more of alcohol than anger. Letting bygones be bygones they would however be needing the body of that nigger so that they could set an example for the other niggers to follow. John told them that he didn't have the body or any information on its whereabouts and even if he did, he wasn't in a sharing mood. Maybe the negroes loosened the noose and removed the body themselves while you were busy chasing me into the bush he said as he stepped from the porch back into his house, closed the door, and consoled his wife.

The mob then went down amongst the blacks and offered a reward for the return of Arthur Edwin's body. When the reward didn't work threats took its place. When the threats didn't work violence took its place. Still no body was produced and in fact the absence of a body had the exact opposite effect of the one desired by the lynch mob. Stories of Arthur Edwin began to circulate far and wide. Fantastic and magical stories of how the spirit of the forest had released him from the noose. Defiant and militant stories of how he'd defied the lynch mob and outwitted the pack. Arthur Edwin became the patron saint of the black oppressed community of Alabama. Late at night when you have no one

32

to turn to and the odds are against you Arthur Edwin will be by your side they'd say.

Person after person spread the legend of Arthur Edwin, told of how he'd spoken to them in dreams, saved them from being raped, saved them from being lynched. The black people in Birmingham felt emboldened; after all they had their own personal savior now, one of their own choosing. Arthur Edwin's absence and omnipresence gave them the one thing the whites had taken from them and hoped to never have returned, hope. And that hope endured in the face of unspeakable atrocities, that hope endured through the lynchings of the 40's, the bombing that killed 4 little girls in '63, through Dr. King's death in '68, that hope endured through it all.

And today while I was working at the polling precinct, watching people vote for a campaign based on hope, a man that appeared to be well into his 90's if not 100 years old walked in to cast his ballot for the first African American to ever be seriously considered for the highest office in the land. His head was bowed and his hands trembled as he filled out the voter information card. Tears fell from his eyes onto the paper smearing the ink a bit. I walked over and asked the gentleman if he was alright. He looked up at me his face streaked with tears and said, yes sir, yes sir I am. I helped him to the booth where he took off his hat, coat and scarf, handed them to me then stepped inside to cast his ballot. His body language exiting the booth expressed his immense sense of accomplishment. I never thought I'd see the day he said. As I helped him put his coat back on I couldn't help but notice an abrasion that circumnavigated the entirety of his neck. My goodness, how did you ever come by such an injury? I asked. His head was held high as I applied a sticker that read I voted to his coat. One night a long time ago, I slipped, he replied then as swiftly as he'd appeared he was gone. Out of curiosity I went over and pulled his voter information card. The one with the running ink, streaked with tears. Guess who it was?"

"Get the f#@k out of here pop pop!"

"Girl what'd I tell you about cussing!?"

33

If You Should Ever Need It [pt 1]

Running in and out of one stops
Buying Now & Laters and Blowpops.
Me and my man, we grew up as best friends.
It seems like we had more in the beginning
When we had less ends
And I guess in the end that's one of life's lessons.
We weren't troublesome
I mean we got in trouble some
But compared to most in total sum
I think we committed less sins.
One night while drinking Wild Irish Rose
Chased with a fifth of Hen
The Bum on the corner
Said, "Look I'm trying to warn ya!
If you ain't careful this thing called life can get away from ya.
Heed a piece of advice tonight from someone who wasted his."
But we were just two wasted kids
Shouting 'til we went hoarse
Playing H.O.R.S.E. on blacktop basketball courts
For the love of summer and the sport
Until our parents called us in.
But summers and the wind
Blow past faster than you know;
And before you know that man in the mirror
Is nearing thirty years old.
We were no longer boys hogging the rock
But fully grown men.
I returned to the block
When I was fully grown when
I'd moved down south and hadn't been home in
About a decade.

And life they say is like a parade,

It waits for no man.

I came home kissed my mom,

Traded jokes with my old man,

Laughed at the young girls

And played chess with the old men.

Then I told them

That this young man's searching for his old friend.

Then they told me

Sometimes your youth can serve as an omen.

They said, "Your man still lives his life like he's on that blacktop court.

He couldn't pass on the rock.

He tried to sell blow but got popped.

He ended up shooting horse."

They said, "We don't know if it's by chance

And we don't know if it's by choice

But now he's that voice

You hear clear down on the corner

Shouting at the kids,

'Be careful or this thing called life can get away from ya

Heed a piece of advice tonight from someone that wasted his.'"

I went down to the corner to come face to face with this man

And came face to face with the face of my best friend

Back when we were kids

And I couldn't believe this face was his.

We both stood there facing tears.

I said, "Look, I'm here and I'll help you get off the dope man

Treat it, beat it and defeat it."

He said, "Look man I've been through three, twelve step programs.

I've advance, I've retreated, I've been defeated."

He said he was going to live and die with a habit

That I could call him an addict

But he was just going to have to be it.
I said, "Look man you're my fam
Until the oceans, the rivers and the seas have receded;
And I may not give you the money you want
To get drunk, high or weeded
But I've got some high tops
And a jump shot on the black top
Some Now & Laters and a Blowpop
If you should ever need it."

CHAPTER THREE

"Not all scars are visible. Regardless, they are usually painful when you first get them. But with time they might fade or they can remain and become a beautiful reminder... that you survived."- José N. Harris

The Talk

Pop walked slowly into the room
Pulled up and sat down on a stool.
I'd just turned twelve
He turned and said well
You're going to be a man soon.
In the coming years, months and weeks
You're going to get off in these streets
And try to do some of the things a man would do.
So let me be clear I want to speak to you here
About some of the things a man should do.
It's time for me and you, to have "The Talk."
Now I didn't buck nor balk
I'd been waiting for this, nay
Praying for this day.
I'd read some books that dealt
And took some notes and felt
I knew everything he was about to say.
I'd read some pleasing words
About the bees and birds.
I'd dialed some numbers I shouldn't have,
Charges and fees incurred.
I hid my brother's Penthouses for him.
I'd chosen my own adventure and read some Penthouse forums;
And I'd venture to say all of this was going on
Around the same time I was sneaking
Into the living room late evening on the weekends
To watch scrambled porn.
Now, scrambled porn was cable porn
That even if you didn't pay for
It still kinda came on.
It was mostly interference and snow.

You'd stare until it cleared for a millisecond or so
Then a woman would let out a low throaty "Oh, oh!"
Then a flash of feminine flesh would ghostly show
And I didn't know if that was an elbow, arm, toe or tit
… but somewhere in my young fevered mind I just knew I wanted to
f#ck it!
But look f#ck it, let's skip to this one week in school
They made the boys take a seat next to
One another
And watch an old movie
About a woman who was by now old enough to be
Someone's great great grandmother.
Here in her youth she didn't have the common sense
To make her lover use a rubber
And she had since
Uncovered and discovered
That she'd picked up herpes simplex 1 through 6!
You can forget
Nightmare on Elm Street, Friday the 13th or Halloween
This was by far the scariest $#!T
My young eyes had EVER seen!
She seemed to have white crusty cauliflower for lips
And her privates nestling just between her hips
Looked like a bleeding, boiling festering oil slick
Several boys passed out, a couple got sick,
One kid cursed his own @ss out for his own wanton wickedness
And promised to never use his never been used d!ck.
After a couple of views
We all vowed that we'd choose to exclude ourselves from sex
We'd become monks next month yes just forget it…
But by lunch we were trying to hunch the girls and play
Hide and go get it … and so that's just how that goes.
But now I'm staring at my dad as he supposes

To lecture on the sexual lexicon
But little does he know it's
Me who is about to get his lecture on…
Every kid wants to impress their parents
So I spoke with hubris
About the pubis and mons veneris.
About the labia
And the way that the
Pubic hair is
Protection.
About erections
When and where it's
Appropriate to display affections.
The clitoris, uterus
The ratio of fellatio
Ejection or ingestion.
Baby, boy or girl
Epidural, c-sections.
Foreskin, foreplay, condoms
Any questions?
Now he's staring at me and I'm guessing I've impressed him.
Then he spoke sparingly and here began the lesson.
He said listen.
This is something you won't learn in school.
This is "The Talk" that all black men have with their sons
… son here are the rules.
The Police can pull you over when and wherever they choose.
Hang your hands out of the windows and make no sudden moves.
Never run from them, their bullets run faster and they are against you.
Never run to them, their laws run slower and they are against you.
They hate black faces, like an angry minstrel
And will shoot you in the back during a chase
Until the pain and blood seem menstrual.

Keep a cigar box filled with bail beneath your bed
For the night that your wife has to come get you.
Know that the law views you as a fool, as disposable
As pitiful, as opposable, as miniscule
And if you ever have a child
You will sit with anger while
You deliver to him the same speech that I have just given to you.
That's something as black man they'll never teach you in school.
Then he stood up from his stool
And left as slowly as he came.
He paused by the door
And said "oh and for sure
Use a condom and don't bring home nothing we've got to name."
I sat there staring at the floor with a look I can't explain
Knowing I'd have to come to grips with this
Live, persist and exist with this
And understand that my real life was scarier than an old flick
With a chick with herpes simplex one through six.

"From what I understand from doctors, that's [pregnancy due to rape] really rare. If it's a legitimate rape, the female body has ways to try to shut that whole thing down."-Rep. Todd Akin (R-Mo.)

<u>Soul Akin [Aching]</u>

She walks into the police station shaken;
Her panty hose and nose running, her mind racing.
Her innocence easy to behold once golden now taken,
Stolen. She walks in holding her shirt
Down to where her skirt once lived.
She's holding back anger, back pain, back tears.
Others are pacing or impatiently waiting in line
To complain,
To report petty crimes
As they smirk, they doubt, they leer, they sneer.
Finally an officer comes out,
Comes over, comes near,
Leans in, comes closer
And says "So what brings you here?"
And through clenched teeth, fears and mascara smears,
Ripped clothes, balled fists, trembling lips
And a torn soul she
Looks at him and says slowly...

"I have been raped."

He turns his head to an angle.
He looks from her foot, to her ankle,
To her thighs, to her breasts, to her chest
Mentally undressing and re-raping her with his eyes.
Then he begins to berate and harangue her.
He asks, "Was it a stranger or were you on a date?

42

What kind of shirt did you have on?
Was your skirt short or long?
Did you flirt, play a long?
Tease, lead him on?
Were you on the make?
This is just due diligence
Make no mistakes miss
I'm not saying you're at fault
I'm just trying to figure out if this
Is a legitimate rape."

And in her mind begins a debate
What in truth constitutes legitimate rape?
Is it housewives
With daggers and fire in their eyes
Taking it and faking it
Their entire married lives
because that's what their mom's did?
Is it forgotten
Little kids on milk cartons
That you'll never know
Snatched from their homes, bus terminals, skid row;
And sold
As sex slaves
In the home of the brave, Brazil, Negril, Russia, Mexico.
Or is it the plight
Of the Native Americans and Australian Aboriginal;
In a fight
In a place they call home
With no place to call home
Just the sight of blight and disease.
Blankets filled with pox to rock their young to sleep
And the memories of Pine Ridge, Hawkesbury, me at Wounded Knee.

Or is it preachers and priests that take liberties
With the least of these.
Snakes that slake
Their desires with the boys choir
beware of the mitre and the muscle T's.
Or at least it must be
The oppression, suppression and stealing of Africa's resources,
Religion, voices and identity.
Could it be building a nation with forced slavery?
Or what the French did to the Haitians in 1783?
What the Germans did to the Jews?
What the government is doing to schools?
What the financial institutions are doing daily to me and you?
What Monsanto is doing to the world's food?
What the pharmaceutical companies are doing to the world's youth?
Don't misconstrue or get it confused
Is this not in truth what legitimate rape constitutes?

Probably,
But could it not also simply be
A woman walking home alone
Not conscious of what she's got on her back;
Thinking she's got the right to wear what she likes
Without being attacked
When she feels a knife to her throat
And her skull being cracked.
Is it rape if she said no, fought and cursed the act?
Is it still rape if she said no but thought not to make it worse and so she
didn't fight back?
Is it rape if she screamed in a way deemed to raise the alarm?
Is it still rape if she spoke softly, in an effort to keep him off she spoke
very calm?
Is it rape if she said no and kicked trying to harm him?

Is it still rape if she said no but since I can't stop you please just wear a condom?

She looks at the sergeant with whom she's lodging her complaint.
His eyes are darting still debating what it is and what it ain't.
She grabs his face and full attention
Pulls him in close to ensure that he's listening
and says "Let me be frank. My rape does not become legitimate when you say so.
My rape became legitimate the second I said, no."

"Domestic violence causes far more pain than the visible marks of bruises and scars. It is devastating to be abused by someone that you love and think loves you in return." -Dianne Feinstein

Foundation

I wonder if it was a man or a woman
That funded the foundation
That founded foundation
So that women all across this nation
Can cover up the pain, betrayal and lies.
I've come to realize
That a wide array of designer shades
Are often used to hide blackened eyes from display;
And that lipstick just the right shade can disguise
And mimic healthy lips once they've been split;
And that blush done just right
Can keep
Bruises on cheeks
Out of sight for weeks.
If you can get the foundation to blend in with your skin tone
Then no one will begin to know the wars you wage at home;
The open sores created behind closed doors.
No one would suppose the hell you've just been through.
Every day, everyday women
With their battle scars hidden
Conduct business as usual.
Sittin' in your cubicle
Your eyes stare at the screen
Your mind replays the scenes
That seem to be
Happening more frequently.
You find yourself seeking the

Answers to the questions "Why is the man I love beating me?"
"Why is the man I married mistreating me?"
And you think back to how what once
Was just a playful childish push
Has evolved into a full grown punch.
Your thoughts interrupted by a co-worker
Who asks you out to lunch.
You politely decline, "Nah girl not this time,"
And you flash her that fake everything is fine smile;
While inside your soul begins slowly crying;
And inside your soul continues slowly dying.
Leaving you relying on strong foundation
To support this house of lies;
As your eyes stare at the screen
And your mind replays scenes
That seem to be
Happening more frequently.
Just the other week in the
Kitchen you limping
From a deep bruise.
Your eyes water as you kiss your daughter
And send her off to school
…like your mother used to do you;
And abuse your mother
Is what your father used to do too;
Like your husband does you.
It's almost as if your mother was you.
Your stories are so similar
They blend into a blur.
In truth in your youth
You learned your make-up secrets from her.
In many situations in more than one way
Mothers lay the foundation;

And lot of girls grow up thinking it's okay then
And it's just that way and
When their husbands start pouring punches
Some women never say… when.
That's when your girlfriend comes back to your cube again
Asking if you're sho' 'cause she's about to go
And you say, "Nah girl go 'head. I'm gone make do."
Then you begin to think, you know what,
She wears her shades inside a lot too;
And her foundation blends in with her skin so beautiful
And you begin to notice this trend from cubicle to cubicle.
On the train, in the store, no matter what you do
You see a nation full of women going through it just like you;
And if it's the last thing you do
You'll make sure your daughter doesn't inherit the secret from you.
The secret that,
A wide array of designer shades
Can be used to hide blackened eyes from display;
And lipstick just the right shade can disguise
And mimic healthy lips once they've been split;
And blush done just right
Can keep
Bruises on cheeks
Out of sight for weeks.
If you can get the foundation to blend in with your skin tone
No one will begin to know the wars you wage at home;
The open sores created behind closed doors.
No one would suppose the hell you've just been through.
Because every day, everyday women
With their battle scars hidden
Conduct business as usual.

Un-fare

Dec. 19th 2014 | 10:15 a.m. | Godby Rd and Old National Hwy | Route 89 MARTA

She boards the bus her eyes fixed on the back seats, her mouth mumbling words meant for someone, everyone and no one in particular. From her lips dangles an unlit Newport that bounces like a symphony conductor's baton as she speaks, the words inaudible. The corners of her mouth point to her feet and her feet stay pointed toward the rear of the bus. She produces a well-worn MARTA card, taps it against the fare collector and begins moving toward the seat her eyes have set their sights and heart on. "Hey. HEY!" comes a call from the bus driver. His words find nothing but the back of her head as she moves steadily away from him. "HEY! You don't have enough money on your card!" She never slows; her head never turns to acknowledge his claim. She moves purposefully toward her goal. "Hey!" The bus driver's voice is all acid and bass. He reaches into his pocket, pulls out a cell phone and begins to dial. The woman settles into the rear bus seat her eyes have never left. Her shoulders relax. Her head rests against the cool windowpane. She closes her eyelids and for the first time since boarding the bus, stops mumbling. The bus driver hangs up the cell phone and shouts, "You either pay, exit the bus or go to jail! The police are on the way!" She opens her eyes and sits up straight. She sits perfectly still as her eyes dance around the bus wildly, a deer in the headlights. The driver addresses the bus "I'm sorry folks we're not going to be able to leave until the police get here!" A gentleman near the front addresses the bus driver "Come on folk! I can't be late again! I'm gone lose my job." The bus drivers retorts, "Don't blame me," as he looks into the review mirror and points at the woman sitting, Bambi in the high beams, in the rear of the bus and continues "blame her!" A lady a few seats behind him turns and addresses the woman "Come on now! Get off the bus!" Others start to grumble and voice their

49

displeasure, their irritation rising. I say to the lady "How short are you on the fare?" In a voice that is more a whisper than anything else she sheepishly replies "The whole thing."

Dec. 19th 2014 | 10:00 a.m. | Flat Shoals Rd and Old National Hwy | Route 89 MARTA [Fifteen minutes prior]

The Route 89 bus rounds the Kroger that sits at the corner of Old National Highway and Flat Shoals Road, and slows to a halt. I'm tempted to wait for the 189, my usual route, but the 89's doors swing open and warmth escapes like it's grandma's oven promising baked perfection. I board the warm bus, on this cold day, with $2.50 in quarters in hand to pay the fare. I tap my card against the fare collector and it reads accepted, denoting that I owe nothing. This is odd. I don't ever put any extra money on my MARTA card. I pay as I go. There is no reason that there should be a free fare on my card, but who am I to look a gift iron horse in the mouth. I tuck the $2.50 back into my pocket, take one of the few empty seats near the rear of the bus and look out of the window.

Dec. 19th 2014 | 10:17 a.m. | Godby Rd and Old National Hwy | Route 89 MARTA [seventeen minutes later]

I say to the lady "How short are you on the fare?" In a voice that is more a whisper than anything else she sheepishly replies "The whole thing." I reach into my pocket remembering the $2.50 still there as a result of my unexpected free ride and say "Here you go, no one should have to go to jail over $2.50." The deer escapes the headlights; her eyes soften and seem on the verge of tears as her hand reaches across the seats and takes the money from mine. A gentleman seated near us shouts up to the bus driver "Hey! Hey folk! She got the money buddy! No one should have to go to jail over $2.50." Funny, I've heard that somewhere before. A few other people take up his championing of her

50

cause. Some of the now champions had just moments before voted with their voices to have her expelled from the bus. It's amazing how quickly tides, ideas and stances can change.

She makes her way to the front, pays the fare and beats a hasty retreat back to her seat. The bus driver pulls the cell phone from his pocket and calls off the dogs. The woman whispers over to me, "Mister, you gave me $2.75. Here's your other quarter." I say, "It's okay, you can keep it." "No sir, I appreciate what you done, it's yours," is her reply "My name is Dometrice." She smiles for the first time, extends her hand and I shake it. I actually already know more about Dometrice than I should. I know her full name, date of birth and according to the hospital band on her wrist, her case number is 1846594. There is a picture of her on her wristband. In the picture she's wearing the same things she has on now. She may have released herself on her own recognizance. She may have nothing to put on except what she is currently attired in. I'm not sure. The one thing I am sure of is that she shouldn't have to go to jail over pocket change.

The bus pulls off and eventually makes it to the station. I ask her if it's ok if I take her picture and share this story. She shrugs. I take the picture. I stand to leave and she says "Mister?" I say, "Yes?" She says "I will take that other quarter if you're not going to use it." I give her the quarter and exit the bus. As I walk to the train I think to myself, what if I had been charged for my ride? What if I had taken the 189? What if... Then I thank God that I hadn't and that I didn't.

Knock knock knock...
Knock knock....

Geezus ... I can hear them moving around inside the house as they try to tip toe quietly, covertly, clandestinely. Unfortunately they're about as stealthy as elephants, goose stepping in jackboots across hardwood floors. To my right the living room shades flutter then stop. To my left a bedroom blind is depressed by a painted fingernail then quickly released. I hear someone approaching, the slap of bare feet against bare floors. I watch as the peephole is eclipsed by the cautious eye just on the other side of the stained birch colonial panel door; scrutinizing, surmising, hiding. I hear two voices begin to whisper,
"Do you know him?"
"No, I don't know him. Do you know him?"
"He's probably witnessing for Jehovah."
"He doesn't look like he's witnessed Jehovah."
I peer futilely back into the peephole, its glass eye blinded as if covered by a cataract from this side and a finger from the other. In my mind I can see the occupants of 2103 Whitcomb Street crowded in the front hall, pressed against the door in their silk-ish pajamas. Bad breath and rustled hair in tow checking each other like hockey players into the extremely thin sheet rock, poorly laid by Home Depot procured, penny paid, border bounding day laborers. The hidden residents jostle for position and a chance to view and disavow any knowledge of this random stranger... of me. I feel sort of like a Peeping Tom in reverse ... sort of. Secretly I hope they don't answer, that the door remains closed, that they continue to whisper in a conversational tone, and question, and eventually tip toe loudly away, bare feet slapping against bare floors. To be honest, I don't want to talk to them as much as they don't want to talk to me. This morning, I don't want to talk to anyone. Finally after a few more painful minutes of "No! I don't know him!" mixed in with an awkward moment of "Are you having an affair,"

which was followed by silence then what sounded like sobbing, I get my wish. I hear their silk-ish pajamas make the sound of material slipping and sliding against material as they retreat deeper into the safety and warmth of their home; a home that apparently serves as a refuge and hiding place from Jehovah's Witnesses; a home that until this morning was happy. Maybe they're in the Jehovah's Witness protection program. Maybe they'll divorce. Maybe they'll work things out. Maybe. I don't care. I walk, not knowing or caring about the course of their future, down their steps made of stone cut in New Mexico and stolen from Argentina. I cross their lawn perfectly manicured by illegal laborers stolen from Argentina and sold in Old Mexico. Firmly mounted in their Crayola Crayon Jungle Green colored lawn is a sign that reads "We Care." I open their gate made of wood cut from the deforested rainforests of the Pacific Northwest, exit their yard and head toward the next, eco-friendly, protected by walls of brick and denial, beware of the dog and the dogged, don't walk on or smoke the grass, no soul and no solicitors, house on the block.

She and I started dating about a year and eight months ago. Her name was Adrasteia, try saying that three times real fast. They say how you start is how you finish and well, we started in a hospital emergency room. There I was, hungry as a Muslim at a noon bar-b-que during Ramadan, and tired as a one armed man with crabs. I was exhausted from grimacing and faking searing life threatening abdominal pains in an attempt to score prescription doses of acetaminophen and hydrocodone. Trying to fool the doctors and nurses at the hospital is difficult but not impossible besides it was safer and way more fun than trying to score on the street. If only all meth dealers were as nice as Walter White... or maybe Jessie... yeah definitely as nice as Jessie. Adrasteia had been giving me the best and slowest hospital service any uninsured, pre-Obamacare citizen could ask for or expect. She had to be the loveliest (and maybe the only) Licensed Practical Nurses Assistant's Assistant (LPNAA) I'd ever met. When I finally worked up

*the nerve to ask her out I could hardly believe she said yes, and I could
also hardly hear her answer over my stomach's grumblings and the
hint of drug sickness that was turning the volume down on my life. I
asked her again just to be sure I'd heard her correctly and that she
truly understood the question,*

"With me!... would you like to go out with me!?"

*"Yes! I'd love to go out with YOU!" she said smiling broadly the white
of her teeth being what Red Riding Hood saw just before grandma
chewed her down to bone and cartilage. Her teeth matched perfectly
with the pristine whiteness of her smock. Few things are that white:
freshly driven snow, a new born polar bear, a can of freshly opened
Crisco, Statesville, GA. Both her smile and smock stood out starkly
against the red blotches and streaks of some stranger's blood painted
haphazardly across her work attire. It made her look like the walking
breathing embodiment of Japan's flag. She continued, "Now, take one
of each of these on a full stomach only when the pain gets unbearable
and don't drive or operate any heavy machinery while medicated.
Okay?" I smiled back at her amazed by my dumb luck and told her I'd
pick her up the very next night for our first date. I popped two pills
right then and there, and grabbed my keys...*

As I walk to the next house, 2105 Whitcomb Street, I realize it looks
just like the previous house, and the previous house looks just like the
previous 10 or 15 houses I've visited today. From shingle, to stucco, to
window, to siding, to foundation it's groupthink the homestead edition.
These people not only keep up with the Joneses they Xerox the Joneses,
create paper cut outs and paste them on top of themselves. It's a
Stepford neighborhood. It's the pod people from *Invasion of the Body
Snatchers* fully realized, with VW Beetles, trust funds, and valium. If
you were the owner of one of these doppelganger dwellings and
someone removed all of the house numbers and spun you in a circle,
once righted you'd be hard pressed to find your needle in this
homogenized haystack. And finally if any inkling of individuality, of

selfhood, of one's unique signature creeps into these Xerox, pod, Stepford, Jones people's minds, The Subdivision Homeowners Initiative Treaty's [The S.H.I.T.] contract of coalescence squeezes and pushes that final ounce of creativity left in the bowels of these parakeet people, out; until anything that says you're different, special, that you're you is just left circling the bowl. You will pay your mortgage, you will conform and you will like it. That is the mantra. That is the discipline. So now this entire community is stuck in their gated, neatly manicured, all cars must be in the garage, all trash cans must be an inch from the curb, all colors must be pre-approved, all fences must be picket and white (white is always pre-approved), boring, monotonous hell of their own floor plan design; and they're paying top dollar for the privilege … As am I.

The first 3 months with Adrasteia were bliss … aren't the first 3 months always though? I call them the Old McDonald days because you prance around the town like stallions, eat like pigs and fuck like rabbits... E, I, E, I, O! She decided that on our first, post emergency room, date she'd lay all of her cards on the table. She wanted no secrets between us. The conversation began as we perused the menus at an Orangewasps. Orangewasps is an Applebee's knock off owned by well tanned white Anglo Saxon Protestants. The restaurant has prices to die for, literally. Orangewasps has never received a score greater than 50 from the restaurant health inspectors and 1 out of every 100 patrons gets food poisoning, it's kind of like stomach Russian roulette or what some call the Orangewasps' emergency room lotto. You just hope your number doesn't get pulled. I would imagine the risk to their customer's health is predicated on the fact that they sell day old expired beef, genetically modified chicken and bleached pork kept in buckets of water on the floor ... E, I ,E, I, O! I'm sure the health inspectors would shut them down if they didn't have their hands and hooks into every level of government and law enforcement in the state. Those orange WASPS always get their way.

The first thing she felt important to tell me was that she had once been arrested for stabbing her ex-husband, although she'd found occasion to stab him more than just once. That diced chicken nugget of information let me know that if this thing between us lasted, if it took its natural ball and chain progression, that I'd be locking up the flat wear and solely responsible for carving the Thanksgiving turkey. There were also a few other useful tidbits about herself Old McDonalded out; "And a sleep apnea here- And an ingrown toe nail there- here a dimple-there a scar-everywhere urinary incontinence." Sing along if you know the words. What could I say? I too was far from perfect. We were both having what the waiter identified as some form of steak when she revealed the coup de grace, the final thing she felt I needed to know before we put another foot forward in this race toward everlasting relations. She had a thirteen-year-old son. She felt like I should know up front just in case I was on a MILF free dating diet ... kid-tose intolerant. I almost threw my napkin on the filthy floor and stormed out of the Orangewasps after being given such news. A slightly homicidal chick with a penchant for knives, that can never wear sandals, snores like a bear and pisses herself when she's startled I can handle; but kids are a lot to deal with. I kept a constant and concrete smile as I steadied myself and let my eyes get familiar with the locations of the exits. Before the flight part of my fight or flight response could take complete hold I figured that in this day and age of tramp stamps, muffin tops, thong floss, condom vending machines and The Real Housewives of Wherever the Hell, if you're not willing to date a chick with a kid you're pretty much relegating yourself to dating fourteen year olds ... And even then the chances of finding one without a kid is 50/50. I told Adrasteia "I think it's great that you have a kid! I mean look at you, I would never imagine that a woman as beautiful and youthful as you are could ever have a thirteen year old anything!" She smiled and blushed and bought it. She went on to tell me that she wasn't comfortable with me meeting her son until after we'd dated for a significant amount of time

56

and decided to get serious. I told her I couldn't agree more. I kissed her and while she wasn't looking went to pocket her steak knife, it was missing. I looked her in the eyes and said "Remember that night that we met? That night in the emergency room." She said, "Yes." I took her uncommonly large hands for a woman in mine and said, "Great, can you drive me back there? I think I just won the Orangewasps lottery."

2107 Whitcomb Street is in foreclosure. The sign out front says there will be a public auction held in a week's time. I walk onto the porch its boards creak at my every step as if moaning about the weight. I look through a window that leads to the formal dining room. I can see a hint of the kitchen just beyond. On the kitchen doorsill I can just make out the marks and names where a record of the height of two children was chronicled. The numbers appear to stop when Justin reached the age of eight and 4' 5", and Sarah reached four years old and 3' even. I'm totally intrigued by this little glimpse into this family's life and almost unconsciously I begin to circle the house looking through the windows and piecing it all together. I begin to see the family's entire story written in the empty spaces; the discolored squares on the walls where pictures once hung, the mismatched rectangles on the wooden floors where rugs used to lay, unpaid bills left to tumble weed about the house, blown by a gust of wind through a window left cracked somewhere.

I imagine a couple lived in an apartment and saved their money. They found a realtor and found this house. They walked every inch of the yard, every corner of the building and they fell in love with it. They agonized over whether they could afford it or not. The financing was tricky and the closing took forever but she covered her face and cried tears of joy into his chest when they were given the keys. The realtor said, "This is your house." His grandma came and blessed every room with holy water the day before they moved in. They made love in every room giving it a blessing of their own the night after. They picked out furniture and hung wallpaper. They had fights and made up. They picked out appliances and laid rugs. They had kids and made vows. They filled this hollow shell with their life, with their laughter, with their dreams, with their hopes, with their triumph with their tragedy with everything that makes us human; everything that makes life worth living. They fell on hard times. They both lost their jobs. The lender was unforgiving. Everyone else was struggling to make ends meet also, so there was no one who could afford to help. The bank finally said, "This is not your house." They explained to the kids that they'd have to move. Leaving felt like having to put the family dog down with a shotgun, but they had no choice. Now this, their love, an empty shell that once hugged their life and kept it from spilling into the streets; this building of brick and mortar that had somehow become flesh and bone to them was being auctioned off. Sold for as little as a person could possibly pay for it. Sold to someone who would not love it, not see it as an extension of themselves but only imagine how much it would bring once gutted, once chopped into units, once section eight-ed, once flipped. And the couple settled back into an apartment and dreamed of falling in love again.

I walk to the front of the house after having circumnavigated its entirety and looked through every window. I walk back up the steps, the boards creaking, the sound seeming different now. Not so much moaning at my weight as lamenting lost loved ones. I know what it feels like to be gutted and left for dead. I knock on the door. I know no one's home. But I do it out of respect for when someone was.

Remember when Adrasteia said she wasn't comfortable with me meeting her son until after we'd dated for a significant amount of time and decided to get serious? Three months is all it takes for time to be considered significant ... three months of getting together, getting out and eating out; and getting together, staying in and eating out is all it takes to get you introduced to a woman's kid. Three lousy months can you believe that!? Hell it took HER nine months to get introduced to the bundle of joy, why am I so lucky? Why do I get fast tracked?

The first three months with Adrasteia had been bliss but as I stood across a mall parking lot looking at her and her son and waiting for the infamous 'meeting' to take place I had a premonition that the best was behind us. And that premonition had nothing to do with the random busty brunette getting into a car somewhere over my shoulder; it was a genuine feeling of foreboding. I could see that her son was just as excited to meet me as I was to meet him as his mother elbowed him in the side and prodded him like an angry steer into coming over and introducing himself. He walked over with his skinny baggy jeans (talk about an oxymoron) down around his knees it seemed, his skull emblazoned bedazzled hoodie swallowing his head, his ears stuffed with noise from his igod, his hands stuffed into his pockets pushing his dangerously low pants down even further and his face devoid of expression. He stepped in front of me, cut his eyes, spit on the ground inches from my shoes and shouted over what he called music "Brent! My name's Brent!" I extended my hand, looked at the loogie near my foot, looked across the parking lot to where his mother was standing, smiled, pulled the ear buds from his ears, pulled him in close, looked him in his eyes and whispered under my breath just loud enough for him to hear, "m#therf#cker."

The owner of the third house on the block, 2109 Whitcomb Street, has left the garage door up. The manila folder colored garage door. Manila folder is not a pre-approved color. You'd think it would be because it's neutral, it's harmless, it's benign, it's…manila. Unfortunately for manila, however, it's too dark to be white and too white to be dark. Manila is a dangerous octoroon. It's the Nat Turner of the Crayola box stirring up trouble. It's the beige-ish bastard telling the rainbow it's not enough. It's Django unchained. We're not even sure it's a color at all and it is definitely not pre-approved. The car in the garage with the manila folder colored door is parked so that the front bumper hangs slightly into the driveway. The headlights lean out as if making sure the coast is clear. According to the Subdivision Homeowners Initiative Treaty, partly in the driveway is not fully in the garage and all cars must be parked fully in the garage when not being actively driven. I have no idea how you inactively drive a car but that is neither here nor there. The trash can at 2109 Whitcomb Street, the house with the manila folder colored garage door, the car not fully in the garage and the vehicle not actively being driven, has to be at least two full inches away from the curb. Two full inches I tell you! The Subdivision Homeowners Initiative Treaty has very clear language and leaves no manila folder colored areas when it comes to trashcan placement. All trashcans must be exactly one inch from the curb. Exactly. And here this person is giving us another full inch. It's almost pornographic in its gratuity. It appears indisputable that the owner of the third house on the block is a rebel; someone that knows that S.H.I.T. stinks. My luck with getting people to answer their door has been none thus far, but if there is anyone and I mean anyone in this neighborhood that's going to answer I'd bet money that it's going to be the owner, I mean rebel, that lives at 2109. I walk up the steps, approach the door and brace myself for the possibility of actual human contact, the real possibility of social interaction not mediated by a wooden door.

Knock …

"YEAH!"

Even after bracing myself I'm still caught off guard by the suddenness of the response, "Uhm… I uh."

"Get the f#&k off my porch! I don't want any!"

The voice from the other side of the door sounds like something you'd expect to hear coming out of the mouth of a Hell's Angel circa Altamont 1969 … which conflicts with the Volkswagen Cabriolet convertible parked one tenth of the way beyond the manila folder colored garage door.

I continue, "Uh … It's good that you don't want any … because, to be honest, I don't have any. My name is…"

"I didn't ask you your fu&king name! Now take whatever pots and pans Amway Primerica Avon Mary Kay State Farm Girl Scout vacuum cleaner Tupperware knives you've got and get the hell off of my porch!"

The very next sound I hear is a loud and distinct click. Now, it could be the click of him unlocking the door, meaning he was coming out to manhandle me off of his porch; or it could be the click of a pistol being cocked, meaning he was coming out to manslaughter me off of his porch; or it could be the click of my own heels backing away from the door, but either way, exit his porch I did.

It's always a tricky proposition to have sex with a woman while her kid is at home. I mean you don't want to stifle yourself and diminish your own pleasure because if you do that then what was the point of buying all of that self warming lubricant and Anal Eze. But with the kid on the other side of sheetrock as thin as Strom Thurmond's skin you also don't want to howl like a banshee, and call her that wildly inappropriate name while slapping her ass so hard that it sounds like someone just broke the sound barrier. Although she loves it when you call her that wildly inappropriate name. It's just not right to mount her like Seabiscuit at the Kentucky Derby and shout like Rick Flair jumping off the top rope, not with her kid in the other room. It's wildly inappropriate. I mean I did it … but that still doesn't negate the inappropriateness of it all. The instant she and I were done making the beast with two backs (the phrase beast with two backs being the only

61

*thing I remember from high school lit) I fell dead asleep. Somewhere
in the night I awoke to go answer the call of nature. I returned to the
bedroom and snuggled up behind her. I know I've sounded somewhat
insensitive during the course of all this but at heart, I'm a spooner. So,
I spooned up against her and wrapped my arm around her waist. Our
hands instantly touched. Our fingers intertwined. Our connection was
so genuine, so easy, so natural. I snuggled in closer I could feel myself
growing hard against her back ready to play another game of "not so
loud/ don't wake my son." That's when I noticed that her uncommonly
large for a woman's hands seemed somewhat smaller, somewhat
smoother; like what could very easily be the hand of a ... thirteen year
old boy! Huh!? I jumped up in the bed stark naked and yelled, "What
the hell!" Adrasteia rolled over naked and startled. The surprise
triggered her incontinence. She shot an inadvertent stream of very
warm and pungent urine at me. Brent lay between us smiling up at me
as urine dripped from my thigh. I grabbed a t-shirt laying on the edge
of the bed, wiped my leg with it and pulled it on to cover myself. "He
had a nightmare and wanted to know if he could sleep in here with us,"
Adrasteia said.
The mistake of donning the shirt I used to wipe my leg became instantly
apparent. "This whole thing has turned into a nightmare," I replied.
She frowned, Brent smiled even wider and said "You're in trouble."
But all I could hear was urine trouble. I put that thought out of my
mind, ignored Brent, looked at Adrasteia and said "Your thirteen year
old hip hop, goth son wants to know if he can sleep with his naked
mother and her naked boyfriend because he had a nightmare? That
doesn't seem odd to you?" Not only did this seem odd to me, I also
knew that those sheets were really not fit for company. Almost every
bodily fluid known to man had touched those sheets this very night. If
they weren't hazmat they were at the very least dangerously close.
"Yes! He has nightmares from time to time and I let him sleep in here
with me!"
"Yes with you. Not with naked US!"*

62

"I'll go back to my room if it's a big deal," he quipped, his eyes all puppy dog, that smile still wide as the horizon. He was trying and succeeding at making me look like the villain in all of this. I could feel the waves of anger radiating off of Adrasteia like Arizona racist Mexican hating heat, so I eased back off of my zero tolerance for thirteen year old boys sleeping in the bed with naked adults policy. "No-no-no, its ok. I mean, you scared me is all ... thirteen huh? ...Well, I mean, who am I to tear a boy away from his mother?" I put on a pair of boxers, kept on the pissy t-shirt and retreated to my side of the bed, letting them cuddle on theirs. It was the strangest night I think I've ever spent with a woman that didn't involve chains, cuffs and costumes. In the morning I roused early and exited the bedroom without waking either of them. While eating the last of the chili con quesos we'd had for dinner the night before I left a note on the kitchen table wishing her and her son the best. I was sure they'd have a great time cuddling and sleeping together well into his 20's, but I just could not be a part of that. It was too strange. Everyone has their deal breakers and for me that was the cigarette that broke the camel's back. I removed the T-shirt and pissed off.

Knock, knock knock ...

2111 Whitcomb Street. A middle aged woman wearing a lingerie set that's more Frederick's than Victoria's, more hood flea market than upscale boutique, jerks open the door, quickly leans forward, sticks her head out and begins scanning from side to side.

"Are you him?" she says.

I look over my shoulder to ensure that no one has magically snuck up behind me.

"Am I who?" It has been a long day and I am sure a bit of irritation is starting to creep into my voice. No one has answered their door and when someone finally does, it's a Madea knock off that is quite possibly in the throes of a psychotic episode.

"Look lady, my name is ..."

"I can't know your name!" She says cupping her hands over her ears and screaming like a child on a plane its ears aching from the changing pressure.

"Just come in," she says as two tabby cats dart out from behind her as if to escape the confines of her madness while a third scampers through her legs and perches himself behind me on the steps of the porch. An odor that's equal parts White Diamond perfume, Jiffy cornbread mix, pig's feet and kitty litter comes drifting from the house. I frown.

"I'm uncomfortable lady."

"Is this your first time or something?" she says, placing her left hand seductively on her hip and using her right to pull at her negligee exposing the mere beginnings of breasts that seem to sag with no end in sight. She smiles a, "you like that don't you" smile and begins to inventory me from head to toe. It's creepy. It's like being checked out by your crazy aunt. Her smile quickly fades and she shouts " … Hey! HEY! Where the hell is your fireman's uniform!? I told them to have you wear a fireman's outfit!" Her face turns red and balls up like a fist at the discovery that I am not properly attired for whatever soul food fire fighting f#ck fest she has planned.

She continues, "What is that? Is your shirt made of flannel? Uh-uh, no way! I ain't paying to be seduced by flannel!"

"Lady! You're not paying me at all!" I reply.

"You've got that right!" she shouts as she slams the door closed, pushing one last gust of pork, feline, cornbread, diamond, feces into my face so as not to forget to also offend my senses. Geezus, you wouldn't believe just how desperate some of these housewives can be. ABC has yet to show ya'll the half of it. I mean I'm not saying she's loose or anything but on my way back down the steps I did trip over her pussy.

The day after the mom/son bedroom debacle I'm at work processing chickens at the poultry plant discussing with Jeff (my not so bright co-worker) the fact that I think the U.S. government's waiting for one of us to die is a piss poor way to gauge the presence and strength of the

64

chicken flu. We're in essence the new Miss Evers' Boys. Jeff stares at me, his eyes blinking very rapidly as if the Apple Macintosh pinwheel of his mind is spinning out of control and he's having a lot of trouble processing the words I've just spoken, before sayin',

"Chicken what?"

"Forget it," I reply grabbing another bird from the conveyer belt and placing it on the hooks.

"Miss Evers' who?"

Jeff typically only speaks in questions, questions that I often treat as rhetorical whether they are or not. I go on to tell him about the night before and the crowded bed I shared.

Jeff replies with more questions, as is his nature "How old is her son again? ... Now, he did what exactly? ... What'd you do?"

I tell him, "I left a note for Adrasteia on the kitchen table, ate the last of the chili con quesos and broke out."

"In cold sores?"

"No! I broke out... I left."

After re-telling the whole story several times and including details that probably should have gone unsaid, I actually felt better. It was the most inexpensive, cathartic, one way counseling session ever.

A little later in the break room is when I first noticed it but I thought it was just my imagination. By the time lunch rolled around however it was clear, people were staring at, pointing at, whispering about and avoiding, me.

Come to find out, Jeff told my story to Myron, who told the story to Anthony, who told the story to Antonio. Antonio translated the story into Spanish and told his girlfriend Consuela. Consuela told Carmen who translated the story into Spanglish and told Juanita, who told Rekeela, who told Tajuana, who told everyone. By the time the story had been told and translated and told again, I ended up naked in the bed with a ten year old boy after using my anus to ease past the sound

65

barrier and covering myself in self warming lubricant, urine and chili
con quesos. Someone called H.R. and someone at H.R. called the
police and before lunch was over two detectives came in and informed
me that they needed to speak with me downtown. The cops spoke like
Jeff, strictly in the language of questions:
"So, do you know the woman and boy in question?"
"So, did you break up with this woman?"
"Did you sleep with her son!?"
"Were chili con quesos present in any form or fashion!!?"
My answers were not as exonerating as I'd hoped:
"Yes, I know Adrasteia and Brent."
"I left her a note saying I was uncomfortable sleeping with her and her
son... wait it's not what it sounds like."
"He and I ended up in the same bed together, but she was there too ... I
mean, we didn't have sex ... I mean, she and I did ... wait, WAIT it's
not what it sounds like! That was before he got in the bed!"
"Yes, D@mmit, YES! I ate the chili con quesos!"
Before I knew it, I'd been booked, bonded, preliminarily heard and was
headed to trial. My public defender's name was Michael Jackson ...
seriously. He looked at my file and said I'd been bad and that the case
would be a thriller but he felt confident that we could beat it. He
laughed. I did not.
Hell hath no fury like a woman scorned, by note. By the time Adrasteia
finished crying on the stand and Brent finished talking about how I was
prone to jumping around naked in the bed and how I had the word
Uranus tattooed on my ass (I know I never mentioned the tattoo before,
it's a lil embarrassing and I was hoping it wouldn't come up in the
trial... so much for wishing), it was a wrap. It was near lunch time
when the jury came back with a verdict of guilty. I was sentenced to
five years but the judge, in his wisdom, suspended the sentence and
gave me probation saying, "Something doesn't add up here; now,
exactly WHO ate those con quesos?" ... I have no idea what it meant

or its bearing on the case. Maybe he was insane with hunger but nonetheless, double jeopardy does apply.

I walked out of the courtroom two things that day, a free man and a registered sex offender. The judge's controversial decision, predicated on chili, sparked a media storm the likes of which hadn't been seen since, the last media storm. I was allowed by the courts to move out of town but not out of the state. The media, hungry for a story, was forced to focus all of their attention on Adrasteia and Brent. Come to find out, Adrasteia was not only the loveliest Licensed Practical Nurses Assistant's Assistant (LPNAA) I'd ever seen but also the craziest Licensed Practical Nurses Assistant's Assistant (LPNAA) anyone had ever seen. Brent wasn't even her son. She'd stolen that boy from a hospital thirteen years ago and was raising him as her own. Before they could get the cuffs on her, she ran out of town too. Crazy.

The only problem with being a registered sex offender, except being driven by uncontrollable passions, that is, if you actually are a sex offender! I'm sorry, I digress. The only problem with being a registered sex offender is whenever you move into a new neighborhood you have to go door to door and disclose to your neighbors, "Hi! I'm a convicted sex offender and I'll be living in the pre-approved white house in the cul-de-sac." As you have seen, the reception is icy at best ... that is of course, when you can get someone to actually answer the door.

Knock knock knock
...knock
I'm almost done, almost informing this block.
...Knock knock...
This is the third to the last house, 2117 Whitcomb St, and it seems like, once again, no one's home. I'm just about to leave when the door swings open. A young man stands staring at me. A familiar voice floats over his shoulder and says, "Brent! Who's at the door?" The

young man looks me in the eye, spits on the floor near my foot and says, "M#therf#cker!"

Adrasteia is faster than she looks. She is at the door before I ever see her coming. I'm cut before I ever see the knife. The door is slammed shut before I ever see it closing. They are both gone before I ever see them leave. I look down and see the bloody knife on the porch it's a steak knife with a handle that reads Orangewasps.

I guess she tried to warn me on our first date about her handiness and willingness to use a blade. My great grandmother always said, "When people tell you who they are, boy you better listen."

So here I am in the emergency room with a knife wound to the abdomen, gutted, hungry as a Muslim at a noon bar-b-que during Ramadan, and tired as a one armed man with crabs. I am exhausted from walking all day, knocking on doors and sort of informing people that I'm kind of a sex offender. The searing, life-threatening pains are probably the only thing keeping me awake. I probably need prescription dosages of acetaminophen and hydrocodone to take the edge off but it's hard to convince doctors and nurses that you're having searing life-threatening pains when you're actually having searing life-threatening pains. That's when I hear the squeaky soft soles of Annie Hi shoes approaching from the rear and the feel of a soft hand on my shoulder. I turn and I'm greeted by a vision in a white and red bespeckled smock. Her nametag reads Desdemona. "I know I'm not supposed to do this but I can see you're in some real pain," she says before slipping me two pills. "Now only take these when the pain gets unbearable okay? You didn't get those from me and the doctor will see you soon." She smiles a wide, gap toothed smile. I take the two pills immediately. They say how you start is how you finish. I wonder if she has any kids.

If You Should Ever Need It [Pt 2]

I saw my fifth grade love
One night in the back of a club
Surrounded by players, pimps, pseudo men... thugs.
I walked over, offered her a drink, some conversation and a hug.
She looked at me, began to blink, there was some hesitation a subtle
shrug
But I pulled up a stool anyhow.
She wore a skirt, a creased frown, a silk blouse, a knitted brow.
Then she said, "Oh! I remember now
That's right grade school!
I remember how
We played hide and go get it
Catch and kiss, that was cool
And I don't mean to be rude
But things are different now.
Dude
I ain't even gone front
Honey it's gone cost you money up front
If you want to sit and chit and chat with me.
I mean $#!t this ain't no Applebee's
But I'm eating wings and drinking daiquiris.
So you can come on and run a tab
Or get gone and catch a cab.
Baby this conversation and time of mine
Are like ladies on the grind at corner of Simpson and Vine...
It just don't come for free."
And me?
I was caught completely off guard.
This wasn't the same girl I remembered
From the springs, summers, falls and winters
On the school's playground yard.

I remember the fifth grade lunch room
Yellow Jell-O, red punch
Her shirt in a bunch
Her hair in a mushroom.
She did the Double Dutch Bus
While I laid the beat to the Krush Groove.
We did all the things that all kids in puppy love do.
I wrote her a note,
I love you
Do you love me?
Check yes [ ] or no [ ]
She wrote in and checked maybe.
We talked in class daily
And while walking home in the street,
Late night on the phone
In our separate homes
Hidden beneath the sheets
Whispering
So just in case our parents were listening
They wouldn't hear us up late sneaking to speak;
Until we both began yawning and blinking, falling asleep
To the sound of a voice, an emotion, a single heart beat.
And maybe that's why I found it so hard to believe
That this woman with her skirt hiked up six inches above her knees
With a tattoo on her right calf that said Ni@@A what!
And one on her neck's left half that read Ni@@a pleez!
That clearly couldn't afford human hair no more
So she had Kanekalon she bought along with some yarn from the
Korean store
Sewed into her questionable weave…
Was the same girl I once knew.
Then she turned and said to me
"Boo-boo

I plan to be the Boss and have Ms. Diana Ross
Doing VH-1 Specials with holograms of Whitney.
I'm going to be on MTV slapping Lil Kim and Nikki on their @ss and
t!tty
While driving drunk as can be like Halle, Paris and Britney."
She said, "I can't floss
With a man that's going to take me to TJ Maxx, Marshalls and Ross;
With a cat standing at the back rack at the Gap screaming, You know
this stuff is 50% off!"
And I said, "Well, I guess all's lost
And there ain't no winning when
The dollars make more sense (cents)
Than the love I'm giving. When
Conversations start coming with a two drink minimum
I know I'm all in
But I fold the hand
I'm giving in.
Because I just can't see it.
We both know I'm one of a kind
But you got a full house in your last divorce
And I guess I just can't beat it.
I may not have the cash you want to get drunk high or weeded
But love I've got that Yellow Jell-O
And a break beat in the lunch room
For the girl I had a crush on
With the bunched up shirt
And the mushroom
If you should ever need it."

CHAPTER FOUR

"Life's Got a Way of Making You Live It."-John E Goode Jr.

Jalopy [Jacob's Story Pt I]

It was in the morning just after Christmas Eve when
All the kids were outside huffing and puffing
On their new ten speeds
Huffys and Schwinns.
They were all thanking some fictitious fat guy
For the gifts their parents went into debt and d@mn near died
To put under the tree Christmas Eve in the den.
This was all gift wrapped within
A celebration for Jesus that Jesus probably wasn't even in
Probably didn't even know about and probably didn't even attend.
Well about three miles away
On that very same Christmas day
In a junkyard that cost about a dollar to get in
There was this little black kid right?
Searching the junkyard back lot for parts
To make a bike.
Truth be told it took him about a week
But he eventually found some handlebars, a frame
Two wheels, two tires, a chain and a seat.
The owner of the lot
Said, "Those little scraps of crap you got
You can have off the yard for free."
So he
Took the pieces home
And began working on
Not so much what it was but what he knew it could be.
This reminds me of southern slaves with hog's guts thrown at their feet.
Their masters said,
"Those little scraps of crap are all ya'll got to eat for the week!"
The slaves knew what it was
But also could see what it could be.

73

So these folks began using the hog's fat for the grease,
And the maw to season the greens
Gathered in teams near the creek.
They put a pot of water on the stove
Added wood until it rose
To a boil from the heat.
They then took the snout, intestines and feet
Flushed them out then let them steep
Until done. Then everyone
Sat the food out and said a blessing over the meat.
The lesson, God will provide
And by God they all had something to eat.
They took food given to them in hate
And intended for their defeat and turned it into a feast.
And as of late
You can walk down Candler Road or any Manhattan Street
And thirty days out of the month, seven days out of the week
Find the descendants of slave owners
Paying the descendants of slaves
Out of their weekly wage
For the opportunity to taste
These so called southern soul food treats.
It's not conspicuous consumption.
It's making something out of nothing;
Just like this kid with the bike frame
As he began
His meticulous construction
Without the aid of inscription or instruction.
That regality cannot be born of refuse
Is a ridiculous assumption.
In reality Joseph and Mary knew a thing
About a king being born in a manger with absolutely nothing.
So I laud this kid's determination

Just like I applaud the gumption
It takes to take a word or phrase
That was used every day and used in every way
To degrade with the presumption
That black meant less that beautiful
Less than smart, less than useful.
A word that made you chattel, made you cattle,
Made you dutiful,
Made you cower,
Took your rights, took your power, took your life.
A word that they
Were going to call you anyway;
And to turn that word or phrase
Into something that amongst yourself says...
You're my brother,
You're smart, Lover
You are poetry, you are art
Above you there is no other.
And to speak this seeming contradiction
With such warmth and conviction
That today the descendants of slave owners
Call themselves this word in their daily interactions and diction;
But when talking to you is when
They suddenly become afraid to use as an addressor
A word used daily by their Klan predecessors
To belittle and strike fear in the heart of your fam's ancestors.
And I know both figuratively and literally its origin is dark;
And that some feel like it regresses us
Stresses and represses us
Depresses and it lessens us
And want it banned from the masses, but me
I can see how they saw it for what it was and used it for what it could
be.

And when the educated African American
Talks about how the word is disparaging, a pariah, a disease
I'm like, educated ni@@a please.
Those people were making dreams out of nightmares,
Creating triumph out of tragedy.
Your hands have never picked cotton
Unless it's for your BVDs or white tees.
Your head has never gotten
Split by a wand, your back broken by baton.
You've never had to flee and sleep high in the trees
Or deep in the reeds
Or been cast from the mast deep into the sea
So maybe know fully informed
On why it was transformed and used
Before trying to say what it should be.
But I digress let me proceed.
The kid took the bike made from the junkyards parts
Sprayed it gold then later rode
It down to the neighborhood park;
So he could play with the other kids
Although in the back of his mind he thought
That they might poke fun, joke, pun and tease.
But they saw the bike for what it was
Beautiful and unique
Not knowing what it used to be.
And he?
He sold that bike for fifty dollars
Made forty nine in profit
And took orders for another three.
He jumped on the MARTA and took another dollar
Down to the junkyard where he was scrounging for bike parts
As it started to turn dark.
The owner of the lot looked out into the yard and loudly barked,

What in Gods name are you doing out there son!?
And he said,
I'm making something out of nothing!
And God knows that's all we've ever done.

What Ya Gone Do [Eddie's Story]

A 22 in his waistband
His face balled up like paper in the waste can.
He told his man he'd case the place
And there is no time to waste fam,
No time to wait and security came on at eight
But took his break kind of late. The plan?
Slam the gun into his face and make him take you to the safe
And then make him open it and take everything that lay within.
Escape into the alley a stolen black Denali
Is what he said he'd be waiting in.
Little did he know, understand or comprehend
That often goes astray the best laid plans of mice and men.

What ya gone do when it all falls down?
What ya gone do when them walls fall down?
What ya gone do when the law comes 'round?
What ya gone do?
What ya, What ya gone do?

What ya gone do when your lady's gone?
What ya gone do when them days get long?
What ya gone do when it's all gone wrong?
What ya gone do?
What ya, What ya gone do?

He thinks on the course that got him there.
His face balled up like beadie bead coarse nappy hair.
Of course his mom and pappy went and got divorced
And he felt forced to make the rent
So he spent his nights with his boys, selling in the stairs.
In the projects is where

They fought for what they thought and were taught was theirs.
Between juve, county and the courts he found himself lost; and here
Comes the night of, black mask, black gloves.
He told his man, you go through the front
I'll meet you in the truck around the back cuz.

What ya gone do when it all falls down?
What ya gone do when them walls fall down?
What ya gone do when the law comes 'round?
What ya gone do?
What ya, What ya gone do?

What ya gone do when your lady's gone?
What ya gone do when them days get long?
What ya gone do when it's all gone wrong?
What ya gone do?
What ya, What ya gone do?

His partner in crime came running out the backdoors
With four bullets in his back near his spine
Shooting over his shoulder backwards.
He jumped in the back just in time,
Just before the gas pedal went flat against the floor.
He had his bleeding back flat against the passenger side door.
When asked what went wrong
He said the safe has a silent alarm
That when tripped alerted another four of five armed to the teeth
Security guards out to catch a thief.
I was lucky to escape alive.
That's what he said just before he died.
That's when the blue lights began to ride
Up from behind and on the driver's side
And all the driver could do was drive

And in his mind try to decide...

What ya gone do when it all falls down?
What ya gone do when them walls fall down?
What ya gone do when the law comes 'round?
What ya gone do?
What ya, What ya gone do?

What ya gone do when your lady's gone?
What ya gone do when them days get long?
What ya gone do when it's all gone wrong?
What ya gone do?
What ya, What ya gone do?

Boosie [Jacob's Story Pt II]

He was raised on assisted living.
T.V. proved daycare
Mother on welfare, father he didn't know
On death row in prison.
On the day of his father's state sponsored lynching
His mother said listen, forget religion
Seek God.
That was the mantra she clung to.
He was given no chances just odds.
One hundred to one
That drugs, thugs and even guns
Would be what he'd succumb to.
Blinded by the stats
That said in fact he'd never see twenty two
Unless tucked in his musty waist band
Along with his father's rusty thirty eight and
As angry as he must be,
His mother said trust me,
Sometimes it's better to walk alone,
Or ride your gold bike
Than to run with your folk.
She showed him an acorn she found while walking home
One night
And said if it stays in the sun
Even the smallest of things can become a mighty oak.
If you lash out and go the fast cash route
You'll never cash in.
You and your friends need to be thinking college
Instead of selling that garbage.
Now go take the trash out;
And be home before the streetlights come on

If you can't get your @ss in, then get your @ss out!

She gave him a rough hug

And said remember YOU are my child!

Not some tough thug!

It was tough love but his mother knew

That the law catalogs your wrongs

And reads you your rights

When you spend your nights

High with your jay crew.

When he saw Justin Beiber beat the rap

His mother pointed at that

And said, don't think you can do what they do.

The difference came the week after his homeboy Eddie got killed

While trying to steal iPhones on the avenue.

His faction turned fraction

After that bullet divided their friend into two.

In addition his girlfriend got pregnant by some other dude

She was only 14 but sum said she multiplied with quite a few.

That very day he started seeing a math tutor after school.

That was 9th grade by 12th his GPA had made

Its way all the way up to a 3.2.

With an SAT score of eleven ninety

He finally got an acceptance letter from GSU.

Four years later he graduated cum laude

His mother sat front row center

And as he and his graduating class entered she shouted loudly

Jesus, look at what God can do!

He handed her his degree

And said it's yours for making me do all those chores,

For giving all those spankings at the time I abhorred

For keeping me above board

When the underground was all I could see

Trust, you earned it just as much as me.

And though tears blurred her sight
She took an acorn she held in her left hand, put it in his right
And said son I know it wasn't easy to trust, believe or please me
But I'm so glad you stayed in the light.
You've become the mighty oak I always hoped you might.
He'd fought the good fight,
Made something from nothing
And thought his accomplishment would somehow in someway mean something;
That the world would speak positively and soundly about his life's decisions
About how he'd cheated death and the way that he'd been living.
He posted a pic on IG so all could see him in his cap and gown chillin'.
It got 4 likes.
The most important thing happening and trending topic in town that night
Was not that a young black man stands as triumph and not victim
… The world was applauding because Lil Boosie had just gotten out of prison.

Room With A View

As a boy, at the end of every summer
Beneath blue skies
His mother
Would take his hand as they ran
From one store to another
A week or so before school resumed.
She'd buy
His shoes a half a size larger than they need be
And purchase his pants a little bit bigger in the waist and inseam.
She kissed him on his head looked him in the eyes and said,
You're a growing boy and you're going to need the extra room.
As a small child he could only assume
That the plan was for him to be
More than he knew, imagined or could see;
That she
Had wishes for her son
As warm as blue skies
And dreams of the man he would become
That were as bright as the moon.

But life will take turns, twists and flips
Do gymnastic acrobatics that in the end
You could never predict
And would have never presumed.

Like for him,
So much hope and promise as he begins…
But then he begins skipping school in junior high
Chasing ends.
As a freshman he got high with his "cool" juniors friends and by
His senior year

He didn't graduate.
He didn't matriculate with his peers.
Instead he was in juve afraid, loud, live,
Mad and unruly just trying to survive.
It's sad, truly, how quickly probation can turn into a three to five.
How a urinalysis violation can make them
Place cold grey bars between you and your warm blue skies.
In the blink of the bluest eye
Less, then more the sun
Sets on an eighteen year old boy, staring in the mirror at a man aged
twenty five.

They killed Troy Davis because they had bigger fish to fry
But for him it's catch and release.
Now he's back on the streets, no GED, no diploma
No job skills and so he
Stands on the corner
Most nights listening to Wayne and Juve;
Rocks in his socks, staring at the sky.
With no bars to obscure the view he
Squints his eyes as he tries to spy
Those things his mother once knew he
Tries to imagine a future as bright as the moon's beams.

In his soul he knows he's not all that he would be.
With his back against the wall he's not at all where he should be.
So he stares intently at the moon and imagines the things,
Imagines the reality of the regality of the king that he could be.
And somehow on his brow
He can still feel his mother's kiss.
So even now
At the end of every summer he still buys his
T-shirts so large that they fall to his thighs

Baseball caps and Starter hats all oversized
And jeans so big, baggy and saggy they fall to the flo'
Because between you and me
I think secretly…
In his mind's hallways he still hears his mother's dreams echo.
Between you and me
I think secretly…
He's still leaving himself room to grow.

The Allegory of the Pot of Gold

There he was standing there
Perfectly imperfect like a fallen Angel.
He was standing at the corner of Candler and Rainbow
Searching for his pot of gold.
Shaking his cup like a prospector
Hoping his dreams pan out;
Thin as a specter
There with his hand out.
He's called a man by none
Son by one
Father by two
By his name by few
And worthless by all;
And worst of all
Is that his rise and fall
Wasn't as epic as Rome's
But equally as tragic.
A stalker of the night, product of a broken home
A creature of habit
Cursed by Catholic nuns in habits
And pitied by Baptist preachers on the Sabbath.
His dreams for the future rest squarely in his cup of tin
And I wonder how many men are unaware that they're in
His exact same position.
I wonder how many men
Somehow have made a way;
With the sweat of their brow
They plow forward and somehow
They've paved a way.
They've paid their way through school,
Worked to stay by payin' dues in the kitchen

And graduation ended those fights with admissions
But real life taught them life's real lessons.
Now those same dudes hold high social positions
And feel like their future rests squarely in their hands.
Just like this man that stands at the corner of Candler and Rainbow
Searching for his pot of gold.

A cold wind gust cuts at his old coat
And old soul.
The traffic light glows red then green
Here come a crowd of people that barely seem to notice him,
That walk past him everyday and act like they don't know it's him.
They act like they don't notice that he's slowly growing thin;
So cold and unforgiving.
They offer cold hard looks but no cold hard cash.
"Get a job and get off your ass!"
A man one paycheck away from the same fate screams as he walks past
And knocks the cup from this man's right hand.
And just right then
I wonder how many men
Are unaware that they are in, his exact same position.
I wonder how many men have climbed the corporate ladder rung by
rung
Until they've come to the top.
Stock ops, expensive living, expensive cars, expensive women
That they lay on expensive linens.
No longer workers but wardens in the suit and tie prison
And that's when it begins.
The sales start to flop.
The market starts to fluctuate.
The bosses start to subjugate.
The stock starts to drop;
And then with a snap

I mean just like that
Hostile takeovers
Downsizing and makeovers
Steal their job and their joy
Knocks the champagne glass from their gilded hand.
And there they stand
Watching their future tumble to the ground
Just like this man that can be found
At the corner of Candler and Rainbow
Searching for his pot of gold.

His cup knocked from his grasp to the pavement
He gasps as he thinks of the days spent
Pulling together a days rent at the shelter
But it's bigger than that, he's been pulling together
A dream of making his life better.
As his cup strikes the curb
The round coins emerge
And spill into oncoming,
And the urge to chase his dream seems
Oh so compelling.
And there ain't no telling him how dangerous this act is
Chasing his dreams into traffic.
And there ain't no feeling like seeing
All your hard work, and all that you've been doing
And everything you've earned
Fall into dirt and ruin never to return.
And there ain't no words
When you see your dreams rolling away fast
Rolling just beyond your grasp
As the world stands on the curb
Slowly turns points and laughs.
Now ask yourself, have you ever been in

This man's position?
Your life's calling seems to be falling by the wayside.
The promises of the twilight have faltered in the night and by the day
they have died;
And you have raged and you have cried against death and living
Staring in the mirror faced with a hard decision.
Do I seek the safety of the ledge? Or do I take the leap?
Riding the razors edge, do I stand on the curb? Or do I take to the
street?
And you're trying to fight the urge
Yet trying to find the nerve to take it there
To make it where eagles dare not fly;
But your dreams are like the Horizon
Right before your sight and you're running as hard as you can
But try as you might
You arms seem too short to ever reach the goal;
Just like his arms seem too short to ever reach his pot of gold.
Broadsided by life you lie on your back and stare at heaven's face
Because only heaven knows how you ended up in the same place
Ended up with the same fate
As the man that stands at the corner of Candler and Rainbow.
And though this may seem strange the allegory's purpose may mean
That some people will die pursing change,
While others are just dying to chase their dreams
… a rainbow… and a pot of gold.

CHAPTER FIVE

"The only person who can pull me down is myself, and I'm not going to let myself pull me down anymore." — C. JoyBell C.

I heard a voice whispering to me in my sleep, in my dreams. It was firm and direct but not panicked. It was a voice I recognized immediately though I could not place it. The voice said,

"Let me tell you a story…

There is a man in a house, a house he did not purchase nor build, but it is without a doubt and with little protest his house. He is neither tall nor short, lean nor fat; he would not be described as handsome nor as comely. His movements through life are sure and pointed but not so hurried as to garner attention. He stands central in every room he's ever entered but shrinks into himself so much that he easily goes without notice. He is average in every way, the exception being that he is ancient. He appears to be neither too young nor too old but despite appearances he is as old as time itself.

This ancient average man is in his kitchen, in his house, preparing a ham. A Smithfield Ham freckled with cloves, swathed in brown sugar, bathed in Coca Cola and haloed with pineapples. A recipe passed down through the family annals with results more comforting than a straw hat and surer than any Straw Poll. As the ham slowly bakes it gives off an aroma that is if not heavenly then certainly just east of Eden. As the ham is pulled from the oven its fragrance, initially trapped just on the other side of the cast iron wood-burning stove's door, wafts lightly through the house. The aroma, a mere suggestion of the ham's promise, becomes an olfactory ocean that high tides its way through every inch of the living quarters, and out of any window left ajar. The smell tempts and entices any that may have the good fortune to encounter it as it dances along the outstretched arms of the mid summer's breeze.

Outside of the house lay Lucky, a dog that the ancient man had stumbled across some time ago and decided to lay claim to. The ancient

92

man had previously owned a dog that had on one occasion broken its chain, tunneled under the fence and run away never to be seen again. Unused to losing things or being without, the ancient man was anxious for a replacement. He stumbled across Lucky in a neighborhood a few miles from his own while visiting on business. Lucky seemed lost, like he was far from home and unsure how to get back. Lucky stood in the middle of the road, thin as a waif, his head swinging back and forth like a pendulum in his confusion. Lucky offered up a few uncertain and tentative steps east then immediately rescinded those deciding instead to go north before instantly thinking better of that and finding himself back at his starting position his head still swaying and searching. He was making an earnest effort to get his bearings and chart a course back home. Lucky seemed harmless, hungry, desperate and determined. The one thing he was, all other things aside, that caught the ancient man's eye and attention, was alone... Lucky was alone. The ancient man enticed Lucky with a piece of ham, a piece of that irresistible Smithfield ham not unlike the one he'd just cooked. Lucky, hungry and lost took the piece of ham offered him in what appeared to be a gesture of friendship. He was quickly subdued, restrained and carted off to the back yard of the ancient man where he was immediately chained to a tree.

Lucky wore a collar around his neck that read Midnight. The collar had clearly been purchased at no small cost and placed around Lucky's neck with both care and an address to which Lucky, re-imagined as Midnight, was to be returned if ever separated from his owner. When the ancient man called for Midnight, Lucky would not respond. The ancient man then decided that Lucky would only be fed when he answered to his recently acquired moniker. It's difficult to be steadfast and hold to one's resolve when you're starving to death. Lucky held out as long as he could then one day barely able to move, he heard the ancient man call out for Midnight. In conflict with all he knew to be right he yelped and crawled as best he could toward the ancient man.

The ancient man patted him on his head, and offered him water and food, he accepted both… along with his new name.

Day and night Midnight dug in his heels his paws tearing away the grass as they tried to gain leverage against the chain that kept him tethered to the tree. Day and night Midnight tested the chain for weak links but it always held. The testing went on for so long and Midnight dug in his heels with such earnest desperation that in time he wore a path clean around the circumference of the tree. The ancient man, however, had learned from the last animal's escape. This chain would hold and never break.

The ancient man knew that life was nothing without hope. He knew that he would never of his own will free Midnight but if Midnight didn't feel he had a chance at freedom then he might not want to go on living. So from time to time the ancient man would add slack to the chain. He'd give Midnight a glimpse of freedom. He'd give Midnight hope. When Midnight, inspired by the added inches to the chain, tried to run, tried to seek liberation, the ancient man would shorten the leash offering Midnight less freedom than he'd originally enjoyed. Midnight eventually learned that while chained he was not to run. Eventually the ancient man, feeling Midnight was tamed and had become accustomed to his station and surroundings, removed the chain completely. Midnight immediately made a desperate dash for the gate, for freedom, but was subdued, savagely beaten and tied so snuggly against the tree he could barely move at all. After a month some slack was added to the chain and in time once again the chain was removed completely and Midnight saw that if he stayed in his place, if he didn't run, he could be free of the chains. He was not allowed to move any further than he was while chained… but he was free.

Lucky, a voice shouted over the fence one day after Midnight had lived for quite some time in the ancient man's back yard. Hey Lucky boy it's

94

me, the voice came again. The ancient man came out of his house and asked the owner of the voice hurdling his fence and sprinting toward Midnight what he wanted. The man said, I think that's my dog. He's been lost for some time but I think that's him. The ancient man said, what's your dog's name? Lucky, came the reply. Oh, said the ancient man, because that there is Midnight. You sure? Was the response from the man still certain that he was staring at Lucky. Positive, said the Ancient Man, go ahead and call him. Lucky! Here Lucky Boy! Here Lucky! The man called earnestly over and over. Sit Midnight, called the Ancient Man and Midnight raised from the ground and sat staring at both men. Down Midnight, the Ancient Man's order immediately complied with. See, said the Ancient Man, Midnight. I guess you're right but the resemblance is amazing, sorry to bother you, were the last words the man said before continuing on to where he was originally headed. The ancient man reached into his pocket and pulled a treat that he tossed to Midnight now oblivious that he was ever anything but. Midnight snatched up the treat, laid down and savored it.

And there he lay again, free in the back yard of the ancient man on the day that the Smithfield Ham emerged from the oven.

As the smell of the ham reached Midnight he rose up and began to yelp, his yelp became a howl and his howl became a growling bark. Midnight himself was probably not aware whether his barking was born of hunger or triggered by the memory of his last taste of true freedom. Whatever his motivation however, bark he did, incessantly even. The ancient man knew that Midnight's barking could not be tolerated; it would not only disturb his family member's rest but it could possibly in time rouse and upset other dogs in the area inciting them to start barking. This would never do. Something had to be done. Finally it dawned on the ancient man that all Midnight wanted was the ham. So he took out a knife and flayed all of the meat away from the bone. The ancient man stepped onto the back porch and threw the bare bone to Midnight. Midnight fell ravenously on the bone chewing away

95

at the cartilage and osseous matter. The ancient man felt assured that the bone would quiet Midnight, cause him to lay back down and be contented. He knew that the bone wasn't what Midnight wanted but it had enough of the taste of what he truly desired to calm him down and shut him up.

From that moment on whenever the ancient man had something cooking up and Midnight barked about it he threw him a bone to quiet him down. This happened with such regularity that in time Midnight forgot that the objective had originally been the ham; he began to believe that the bone had been the goal all along. And when the ancient man walked in measured steps not too quickly and not too slowly over to where Midnight lay docile and unchained, patted him on his head, fed him the bones and said, good boy; all Midnight could think was, "he sure is good to me."

I woke from the dream with a start, the date was September, twenty first, two thousand and eleven. Fortune and fate found me in Atlanta giving poetry performances at local colleges and universities; and though the oppressive Georgia heat often times doesn't subside until well into October, there was something else in the air making everyone uncomfortable. Making everyone sweat. Hanging over the state, heavy as Savannah humidity and thick as backwater buttermilk biscuits was the pending execution of Troy Davis; a possibly innocent black man scheduled to be put to death by the state of Georgia that very evening. Troy Davis was a name that in recent years I'd come to know as well as my own. I'd signed petitions, been to rallies, marched, posted information on social media websites, written letters and emails to the district attorney, the assistant district attorney, the governor, the current POTUS and former Presidents, basically anyone that would listen in an effort to secure a new trial for Troy. I'd worn buttons and t-shirts and held up signs and placards that stated that in all actuality I was Troy Davis. This was an action and sentiment shared and espoused by many,

96

especially people of color in the south; and rightfully so because we knew that the story of Troy Davis could very easily be the story of any of us and the justice or lack thereof that Troy received could be metered out just as easily also. So as we fought to save Troy, we fought to save ourselves.

With no physical evidence linking him to the crime Troy was accused and convicted in 1991 of killing Savannah, GA police officer Mark MacPhail. The prosecution relied exclusively on eyewitness testimony and circumstantial evidence. Seven of the nine eyewitnesses would later recant their testimony sighting reasons as insidious as police coercion. So much of the "evidence" used to convict Troy was called into question that a public outcry rose for a new trial. Some yelled, "Free Troy Davis!" I was still unsure as to his guilt or innocence but it was clear that so was the state of Georgia and so a new trial seemed clearly in order. A new trial was demanded. But to that point none was given. It was clear to me that I was going to have to go down to Jackson, GA on the day of Troy's scheduled execution and have my voice and opinions expressed, if not heard, on the issue.

When I awoke on the morning that the state was to kill (some would say murder) Troy Davis, I had ham for breakfast. The smell briefly returned me to the dream, to that voice, to Lucky. My phone rang before I could fall too deeply into the abyss of that thought; it was my homegirl Naja asking if it was still cool if she rode along with me down to Jackson, GA. I told her absolutely, I was more than happy to have someone along to face the daunting day and Herculean task that lay ahead. Misery and ministry love company.

I borrowed my sister's car and would have to return by 5 p.m. to pick her up from work. I was determined to stay at the prison as long as I possibly could and then return back to the prison after dropping my sister safely at home. The execution if not circumvented by the

governor or direct divine intervention was scheduled for 7 p.m. I
scooped up Naja and we made our way down to Jackson, GA to the
Georgia Diagnostic and Classification Prison. The prison's name
sounded like something out of a Terminator film. It was a name more
ripped from the pages of science fiction than cemented in the hills of
rural Georgia. The prison's title spoke more to experimentation than
rehabilitation, and after looking at Georgia's track record of
rehabilitation vs. recidivism the name seemed to be apropos. Naja and I
listened to music and spoke of benign things as we traveled southward,
in what I believed was an unconscious effort not to stare at the elephant
in the death chamber. We passed road sides that had been worked on by
black men on chain gangs; towns where once cotton was king and
enslaved Africans its oppressed subject. We passed red clay hills that
have drank deep into their memory the blood and spirit of our
forefathers; so much so that our double helix will forever figure eight
through their rolling hills. Georgia's peaches will forever taste of our
storied past. When the wind blows through the trees and the leaves
sway along its currents you can almost hear a roll call of the fallen, the
murdered, of the lynched. If you listen close enough you may soon hear
Troy's name, listen even closer and you just may hear your own.

We arrived in Jackson at roughly 11:15 a.m. and discovered that we
were the first in attendance. There's nothing like being early to the
prison execution party. We were so early in fact that there was still
some discussion amongst the correctional officers as to how things
would be handled (who to mace, who to hog tie, you know the
incidentals...). A short African American woman, who seemed to be
half tree trunk and all mouth, circled to the passenger side of the car,
put her limb on the roof and told us to hurry up ... and wait. Her
directions and demands were so disjointed and erratic at one point in
my mind I literally questioned her sanity. Maybe just maybe being a
participant in the states attempt to kill a man that could be her brother,
or son, or father had caused her to take leave of her senses. The tree

98

trunk's partner a more pleasant brown skinned African American woman sporting freckles and a bullet proof vest approached us from the driver's side. We were being flanked. Freckles kept using both of her hands to pull her bulletproof vest forward in what seemed like an effort to ventilate. Maybe just maybe being complicit in the correctional facilities possible murder of an innocent man had made it hard for her to breathe, had lit a fire in her chest that was growing by the minute and threatening to burn her spiritually, morally and ethically down to nothing. Freckles also decided to place her arm on the roof of the car and lean heavily upon the vehicle. She stared at us for a while, until the silence grew pregnant and awkward like a fifteen year old trying to find the words to explain the spreading bulge in her belly. After the long pause Freckles sucked her teeth and asked what I felt was an amazingly odd question. She asked if we were "For" or "Against." Initially I couldn't fully understand the question. It was just three words hung out to dry without any indication of all that went into the wash. For or Against? My honest feeling was that we were both, we were for Troy Davis living and we were against Troy Davis dying. Was that even the question being asked? For or Against? For capital punishment or against it? For Troy Davis or against him? For justice or against it? For the McRib or against it? What was the question at hand? I clearly lived in this thought for far too long and my answer did not come with the anticipated or desired speed. Officer tree trunk on the passenger side who was getting crazier by the moment (which is scary because we were the first people there so by 3 p.m. or so she would be mad as a hatter) looked past Naja, through the car, stared at me with eyes that have clearly seen horrors that her soul has yet to process or make complete sense of, and said with all due seriousness and volume, "For or against!?" I assumed she meant for Troy Davis or against him and I thought to myself what a question to have to answer. If you had come to the prison with the desire to see Troy executed, to have to say out of your mouth and acknowledge aloud that it is your earnest and heart filled want to see another human being killed, must be something. It must say something to and about you. I told her that we were against Troy Davis being put to the death. This is a statement that she heard as, we are against YOU. This is a statement that I meant as, we are against injustice. This is a statement that signified that we are against the wall, our collective backs still scared from the whip's lashes, our necks broken from the whiplash of trying to watch and follow the latest trends; blindfolds cover our eyes as the firing squad raises its rifles, blinders cover our eyes as we tunnel vision our way through life. We are pressed against bricks made with our own hands. We are imprisoned because of bricks sold with our own hands. I'm not sure if all or any of this was captured in my "against," but that's how I meant it. The officer's top lip curled almost imperceptibly. She did not speak another word to me. She began processing us into what had been designated as the proper area for those "against." Our I.D.'s were taken, our names were written on a log sheet, a lime green ribbon was placed around our wrists (as if this execution was being sponsored by Sprite), a lime green piece of parchment was placed in the window of the car, we were handed a set of rules and pointed forward. Upon pulling forward we were met by another group of correctional officers and instructed where to park. We exited the vehicle and were immediately met by our third and what clearly seemed would not be our last group of officers. This time they came bearing dogs. Dogs on chains. My mind returned briefly to the dream, to Lucky. A growl deep in the throat of one of the dogs immediately pulled me back to the present. Somewhere deep in my spirit I knew that growl, a part of me that I didn't even know existed, a part of me buried deep beneath old fears and antiquity's bogeymen recognized it clearly. I surveyed the scene and mentally ran through my *1963 Rural Alabama Jim Crow Protest Rally Crowd Control Check List*: Dogs *check*, blatant intimidation *check*, cops *check*, batons *check*, civil rights violations *check*, the only things missing were horses, hoses and George Wallace... but the day was young, any and all (save George Wallace of course) might make an appearance before days end.

100

Naja and I brought along our backpacks that contained water, food, notebooks and cameras (nourishment, words and images, the artist's trinity). The group of officers taking their dogs for a leisurely stroll amongst the Negroes, paused, cataloged our belongings and told us that there was no problem with the items we had. We were instructed to move forward, speak with what would be the fourth group of officers we'd encountered since driving onto the prison's premises and to enjoy our protest. We approached the fourth group of officers a few seconds later and were greeted with "What's that a bag?" "What's in that bag" "Is that nourishment? Is that a notebook? Is that a camera? (… is that the artist's trinity!?)" We were informed in quick order that none of that would be allowed. It presented a danger. Food, water, notebooks and cameras presented "a danger?" I wanted to point out that nothing we had was more dangerous than let's say an ELECTRIC CHAIR, but I didn't see what that kind of critical thinking would gain me at that point. The officers seemed to be itching for a reason to remove any and all "against" from the premises. We were told we could take the items back to our vehicle OR leave. We took the items back to the car, walking past the K-9 Keystone cops that told us it was all good just a moment earlier and seemed to be chuckling to themselves now. We returned to the fourth group of officers, free of our dangerous items, and were directed to an area they'd dubbed "The bullpen." I imagined that in this bullpen scenario we were not to be the matadors.

The bullpen was just a roped off area of open grass with three picnic tables within its confines, no shade over head and a huge anthill at the north east corner. I estimated that it could hold comfortably roughly 180 people, so long as no one accidentally stepped on that anthill. Once in the bullpen I took full note of the surroundings and happenings. The officers by our car had the K-9's sniffing the vehicle for what I could only assume was dope, guns, ladders, ropes, cakes with hacksaws inside and Jesse Jackson concealed in the trunk. A group of roughly ten officers only a helmet and shield short of full riot gear stood huddled near the far end of the bullpen. They whispered and looked over at us like bullies on the playground planning to take our lunch money. One couldn't help but notice that 80 percent or more of the officers we'd encountered so far were African American. What a position to be in. Another officer in a polo shirt and khakis walked near the table where Naja and I had settled. I extended my hand, introduced myself and asked him what the protocol was for today. He took my hand, took my name, gave me his and took a seat. He seemed almost relieved that the conversation was not instantly contentious and offered us some insight into how he felt the day would go. He said, "We want everyone to get what they came here for," which I instantly knew was impossible. Some people were coming to see the execution stayed and some were coming to see revenge dressed up as justice metered out. If only everyone could get what they came here for. If only the family of Officer MacPhail could leave feeling that their revenge was exacted and their pound of flesh extracted. If only the supporters of Troy could leave knowing he was safe and justice would be served, not just for Troy but for us all. Ah, if only. The officer went on to say that we would not be getting any closer to the prison than we already were. And we were already so far away from the prison I was unsure as to exactly where the prison was. The bullpen was just beyond the entrance to the prison's grounds. The prison itself seemed to be down a road that could have led to Narnia or Oz (prison irony there) as far as I knew. He continued by saying that once we left the bullpen for any reason other than to use the port-a-potty directly adjacent to the bullpen we would have to leave the premises for the day. He stood, shook my hand, wished me a good protest (the second time that day I'd been wished a good protest) and went over to the corner where he immediately started whispering and looking back over his shoulder at us with the other bullies.

102

Naja and I were talking to a couple that was very involved in the Oscar Grant protests in Oakland when the buses from Atlanta arrived and parked across the road. Even from the distance we sat we could see the sun bouncing off of the crisp suit and bone straight perm of the Reverend Al Sharpton. The groups of supporters or against-ers from the buses crossed the street, protest signs and banners in tow, chanting "I am Troy Davis," the Reverend Al Sharpton at the lead. The officers in the bullpen hastily dispersed like football players running from a huddle ready to play ball. What, if any, infinitesimal sense of friendliness they'd previously possessed eroded immediately. It was game time and game faces. The Reverend Al Sharpton walked into the bullpen, his shoulders as straight as his hair, his head raised high, his voice booming "I am Troy Davis!" A general leading his troops to war. He strolled straight up to me, shook my hand and said, thank you for coming. I knew that he didn't mean me specifically, he had no idea who I was as an individual. He meant the all encompassing "me," the "me" universal. I looked at the ranks of followers quick on his heels and realized that 80% or more of them were women. I then wondered if he meant thank you, black man, for coming. I tabled that thought, looked at him and said, I appreciate you bringing attention to this issue. It was an interesting and unexpected response and moment for me. I sometimes have mixed feelings about Jesse Jackson and Al Sharpton, their motives, and agendas, but in that moment I realized that I do, however, appreciate the attention they draw toward issues that would otherwise go unnoticed. The Reverend Sharpton and I shared another firm handshake and not another word.

I began to see faces from Atlanta that I recognized emerging from the buses; Icy Chevell, Indigo Priestly, Ingrid Sibley, Alicia Waller, Baritone Scholar. They were welcomed sights that offered hugs and words of encouragement. Rev. Sharpton moved everyone into a circle and encouraged everyone in the gathering to respectfully speak his or her mind. This is where things got … interesting. Agendas beyond

Troy's case were certainly pushed at times (some people talked about everything from hocking Noni Juice to selling pre-paid legal services) and grand standing certainly reared its verbose head. A woman in a zebra stripped skirt gave an impassioned speech about how her son endured some of what Troy was enduring and how we must stand up and make our voices heard. It was one of the, if not the, best speeches given. Her speech ended to rousing applause. A gentleman in a leisure suit and Kool Moe Dee shades gave a speech that I must admit was mostly lost on me; he mainly used words that didn't mean what he thought they meant to say things that were not entirely clear to anyone. Excluding the female guard I encountered upon entry, his was one of the, if not the, most confusing speeches given. His speech ended to intermittent golf claps. Later I saw the zebra woman and leisure Moe Dee exchanging heated words about the content of each other's respective speeches. It seemed an odd place to argue about something not truly germane to the issue at hand. It seemed in poor taste. Every so often, back in the circle, someone would break into a Negro spiritual meant to put us into the 1960's protest mood; And that is exactly what it did, but unfortunately it is 2011 and some of that was lost on those of the newer/younger generation. In the 1960's all we had was each other to cling to, the thought was fall as individuals or rise as a people. In 2011 these things were still true but we had the illusions of social media to keep up with, time monopolizing gadgets to purchase, the comforts of our growing middle class to placate us, bank account balances to maintain, the pipe dreams of movies and rap music fantasy to make us feel like we had made it. We no longer felt like singing, "We Shall Overcome," we had an African American man in the white house ... we had overcame. So we thought until a story like Troy Davis's or Sean Bell's or Oscar Grant's pulled our heads from the clouds and rubbed our noses in the stench of our ever present oppression. The beauty of the rally was the brutal reality check, it was the real time, up close and personal fellowship with one anther, the civil disobedience, the sharing of concerns about Troy and the future; it

104

was the genuine bonds made under the worst of circumstances. It was great to see so many people of color, and people sympathetic to the cause gathered, fired up and working together in an effort to collectively find a solution to a problem that has the potential to affect us all regardless of race.

Then the correctional officers began to do what they are paid to do, make things difficult, make things uncomfortable. The sun came out, bright and strong, and everyone immediately realized that the bullpen was in the only spot on the property free of shade and protection from the elements. Consequently folks wanted to get water from their cars or from the store across the street and the guards said, you're free to go but you can't come back. Diabetics and folks that must take their medications with food wanted to return to the bus to grab a sandwich or go across the street to grab a bag of chips and the guards said, you're free to go but you can't come back. The guards were true to their word, when people did leave they were not allowed back in. I also noticed however that people who had never been admitted were not allowed to enter, there is no one for one swap. The guards said they'd admit 150 people and what I soon discovered was that once they'd checked 150 people in on their log sheet that was it. If 150 people entered and 100 people exited, leaving only 50 in the bullpen they weren't going to admit another soul. They would say that by their count 150 people were present in the bullpen and they had the names to prove it.

The people endured however. Some left. Most stayed. Speeches were made. Cameras appeared from what seemed to be smaller independent networks. You would see a CNN every now and again, for the briefest of moments. The day marched forward.

As 4 p.m. approached I knew that soon I would have to leave. I had to drive to Atlanta to pick up my sister from work and my nephew from school. I was torn. I was reluctant to leave knowing I wouldn't be allowed to return. I shook a few hands, hugged friends old and new, encouraged people and made my way to the car. On the drive back Naja and I discussed Troy's case, the beauty of the gathering, what we felt went right and what we felt went wrong with the rally. I dropped Naja off, picked up my sister from work, my nephew from elementary school and continued home. It was my sincere prayer and earnest hope and desire that Troy Davis's life be spared by the state of GA or that the Supreme Court would step in and stay the execution. In a nation that has openly executed the Oscar Grants, Sean Bells and Amadou Diallos in its ranks, and imprisoned the Assata Shakurs and Mumia Abu-Jamals of its citizenry, and openly abused the Rodney Kings and Abner Louimas in its care, Troy Davis represented a chance to get it right. Troy Davis represented a chance to point the ship in a new direction and stand firmly upon the promises and decrees of justice and liberty committed to by the Constitution.

I returned home at 6:30 p.m. turned on the TV and started flipping channels looking for information about what was going on in Jackson. I discovered that at 6:30 p.m., 30 minutes before what in my mind was one of the most hotly debated executions in recent history; 30 minutes before an execution that had elicited pleas of mercy and leniency from the likes of The Pope, Bishop Desmond Tutu and former U.S. President Jimmy Carter … there was no major media coverage of the event. None. I flipped channels like a kid with ADHD and spasms in his thumb but to no avail. When Casey Anthony was on trial (a trial that I might mention freed a woman whose guilt was so apparent that your eyes would have had to be in your foot not to see it) it was impossible to get away from the televised reports on her case. But on the eve and hour of Troy Davis's possible execution the American news media was suspiciously silent. So silent that their message and commentary on who and what was newsworthy rang out loud and clear (your ears would have had to be in your foot not to hear it). At 6:50 p.m. a local station picked up the coverage and I watched as people I'd until recently stood shoulder to shoulder with openly cried, and prayed, and hugged each other hoping for a miracle as the clock ticked down to nothing. At 7:00 p.m. I bowed my head. I knew that at any moment the official time of death would be announced and once again a black man whose guilt was shrouded in doubt that was beyond reasonable would have been killed by the state of Georgia. My eyes returned to the TV and just beyond the reporters off in the background I saw the people who came to plead for justice for Troy Davis erupt into cheers. I had no idea what was going on but I could feel myself begin to smile, a wave of optimism took over and I stood frozen waiting to find out what they already knew. The reporters turned to face the crowd, also baffled by their jubilation. No one in the news media seemed sure as to what exactly was going on, and no one was making an effort to inform them. Then the word came down, an announcement was made, Troy Davis had been granted a reprieve. A reprieve from execution! Tears of joy and amazement escaped my eyes before I could even fully comprehend or be fully informed as to what a reprieve from execution meant in exact terms. All I knew was that for now Troy Davis was alive, that at 7:00 pm the doomsday clock had struck to no avail. I couldn't believe it! In as much as I wanted the U.S. to do the right thing, and in as much as I prayed it would, I don't know if in my heart I ever truly believed that it would come to pass, and there it was, the impossible achieved. I went downstairs and hugged my sister and my nephew. As I hugged my young nephew I thought to myself, perhaps it will be different for you; perhaps justice in this country will finally mean more than Just Us. Perhaps. The details of the reprieve were revealed. Seven days. The Supreme Court had seven days to review the details of the case and to decide if a new trial was warranted. Seven days to get it right. I was drained from the ups and downs of the emotional roller coaster ride I'd endured that day (I couldn't imagine how Troy must have felt). I ate dinner and around 10 p.m. I fell asleep feeling accomplished, feeling victorious, feeling encouraged about the direction the nation was headed in by making the decision to at the very least give the case time for another impartial review. I vowed that in the morning I would take up the fight again, write more letters, send more emails. I was but one voice but I'd been told that enough voices joined in chorus could raise a song that would bring down the walls of Jericho!

I woke the next morning around 6 a.m. My phone was filled with text messages:
"I thought they were going to give him seven days…"
"What happened to the reprieve?"
And the one that knocked the wind from my sails:
"Jon they executed Troy at 11:08 last night."
Seven days turned out to not even be seven hours. In a cowardly, cruel and unusual act, a reprieve was granted the night before stating that the Supreme Court would take another look at the case and just over four hours later, not enough time to even give a tertiary glance at something so complicated, Troy was murdered by the state of Georgia. I felt angry. I felt deceived. I felt an overwhelming sense of sadness. I logged onto the internet and read about Troy's final hours, his last statement professing his innocence and the forgiveness offered to the guard administering the lethal injection. In death he seemed more relevant to the media than in life. I watched the videos on Youtube of the correctional officers in full riot gear taking protestors into custody outside of the prison. It seemed that in the hours after I'd fallen asleep the wheels had once again come off of the freedom ride. A friend that knew I went down to Jackson the day before sent me a text to make sure I was alright. I told her that I wasn't alright but if she was asking if I was safe, I'd indeed left before the cops attacked the crowd. Her response was, "You're lucky."

I immediately thought back to that voice I heard whispering to me in my sleep the day before. That urgent and direct voice that I could not place … and I realized it was my own. In my mind, clear as day, I could see that dog chewing on that bone. I could not help but to think that the goal has never been to sit at the front of the bus, or to sit at a desegregated lunch counter or to share toilets with white folks. Those are bones we have been tossed along the way to see if we'd calm down, be placated, shut up. We've been tossed so many bones that in time we have forgotten that the true goal is, was and has always been equality! The true goal is the right to properly educate our children, prosper and flourish without being murdered. The true goal is to not have a cigar box beneath the bed labeled bail money. The true goal is to not have the hairs stand up on the back of your neck every time a police car falls in behind you. The true goal is to not have to leave instructions on how the family is supposed to survive without you when going to court for a minor infraction. These are but some of the TRUE goals; and we have far and wide missed the mark. We have fallen tragically short of the goal. Instead we walk in our well-trodden circles, relishing our illusion of freedom, scared to death to run toward what we really want and praying for more bones. I looked at my phone and I responded to my friend, "Unfortunately… we are all Lucky."

Over killed [Even if We Concede the Point]

I had a chance to speak with Ebony Janice back a few weeks.
She said I think that we as a people suffer from PTSD,
We've seen so much tragedy and evil we can barely process it or speak.
People speak of slavery like it was some ancient land's mystical beast
But if you look closely at yourself you can still see
The marks of the shackles on your own hands, wrists, ankles and feet.
And the stench of the oppression served daily that they want us to eat
Reeks of hog ears, pig intestines and lungs
Dogs, fear and pigs in vests with guns;
A nation that cares little about the education of our daughters and sons
But has interests abroad and invests in guns.
Jobs, clothes
Gadgets, cars and elevated roles are the dressing that's supposed
To make the dark tart truth taste sweet.
They've got a thousand virgin islands undressing
Your sons still working in fields
And your daughters twerking in the street.
The lesson is oppression's
Deceit is in convincing the oppressed it's lessened or gotten weak.
An older gentleman in the chess park
Offered some food for thought
That he said maybe I ought not repeat.
He said, how are African slaves so hurt, huddled and afraid that they
don't speak
Any different than African Americans that think they've got it made
So enslaved to positions and their comfortable living conditions that
they won't speak?

So let's speak of Justice and I trust this will not fall on deaf listeners:

If Emmett Till did whistle at a white woman, or said something he
shouldn't have said
Did he deserve to be dragged from his home
Shot, alone, wrapped in barbed wire and thrown
Into the Tallahatchie's riverbed?

If Oscar Grant had
Started a fight that night on the BART train
Once subdued and no longer a threat
An officer with his knee on his neck
Did he deserve to be shot in the back at point blank range?

If Rodney King was driving drunk and deranged
Trying to evade police
On an LA interchange
After being captured
Did he deserve to be beaten and battered in the street?

If Trayvon Martin had been suspended for smoking weed
Did he deserve to be stalked
As he walked home
With a phone, tea and candy
Then confronted and shot by a lone vigilante?

If Eric Garner had been selling fifty cent cigarettes
Did he deserve to be choked to death as he begged for breath?

If Mike Brown did steal some White Owls, Swisher Sweets, Black and
Milds
Did he deserve to be shot six times while surrendering with his hands
up?
The bullets entering, two in the head, four to the gut.

And what do we say about Sean Bell who was killed with no "and even if he was"
Or Kathryn Johnston who was killed with no probable cause
Or Timothy Stansbury who was murdered though he had broken no laws?

And now you can add Kajieme Powell, John Crawford and Tamir Rice to the murdered roll call.

Jon is not so green as to believe that the fault is in our stars
But they want to convince you and me the fault in fact is ours.
That racism is an illusion that we're using
As an excuse when
We point out the true sin
Is that it's the builders of this nation,
Laborers, breach birthed unfortunately
That face incarceration
And sit disproportionately behind bars.

So I was blessed to speak with Ebony Janice back a few weeks.
She said I think that we as a people suffer from PTSD.
That we've been over killed, it may sound like overkill but it's not over still.
How do we get off the ground when they stand on our shoulders still?
How do we get over Brown when we're not even over Till?

"A black woman is like coffee. You never know how strong she is until you get her in hot water."-Unknown

Dark [A Dedication to African American Women]

No matter what kind of dating you get into
I'm not the one hating on you.
You've got to do what you do.
This day and age you've got to love who loves you.
But as for me
I love to see these women that are … dark.
I mean dark as an African tribal dancer
Standing on the tropic of cancer
During a lunar eclipse
On the summer solstice
Behold this soul sis.
She's dark as the singers of mid sixties soul hits.
She absorbs everything around
Like black holes or black hands
Holding Bisquick biscuits
Sopping up fish and grits.
In other words, she's attractive.
She proceeds with progress with no stress
She's proactive … and she's dark.
Dark, well rounded and well grounded
Like the bark and roots found in the history of old oaks
That may bend in the wind but never broke.
Dark, well rounded and well grounded
Like the bark, roots and history of old black folks
That may bend in racial winds but never broke.
Dark as the night that slaves took flight
From murderous cotton fields
Where they were whipped raped and killed.

113

God their rod and the darkness that envelopes them their shield.
God their rod and the darkness of melanin their shield
…God knows I love 'em dark.

Dark as the world through the closed eyes of a fetus.
Dark as the world through the open eyes of these elitist.
Dark as the open lies that certain institutions have tried to feed us.
Dark as scriptures descriptions and depictions of Jesus.
Dark as the history of Uncle Tom, Uncle Ben and Uncle Remus.
Dark as the audience that was there
The night I came to hear
Nina Simone sing, "Black is the Color of My True Love's Hair."
I'd like her to be so dark in fact that if she were to lay on black sheets
You'd have to question if she was there!
I love 'em that dark.

Dark as dirty oil.
Dark as fertile soil.
Dark as the prison population down in Macon.
Dark as the past we just left and the future we're facing.
Dark as the patrons who stay in the establishments of government
agents.
Dark as the mental outlook of kids hooked on Playstations.
Dark as the heart of a racist instilled and filled with hate.
Dark as those dudes in dashiki's, that ironically, mostly white girls
date.
Dark as that coffee looks that they've got in the office.
Dark as my finances look ever since Bush … got in the office.
Dark.

Dark as the grand motherland.
Dark as my grandmother's hands that clapped in church on Sunday
morning.

Dark as Hawaiian coasts that boast of black sands.
Dark as the glove held high above by black Olympians
As they took the victory stand and throughout history took a stand for victory.
I like the skin on these women to be so dark you understand
That white women trying to catch a tan cannot help but hate it.
I like these women to be so dark they could go to funerals naked.
I mean darker than the deepest depths of a well.
So dark Satan would look at her and say "You are black as Hell!"
I mean say, hey
If you're into interracial dating I AM NOT hating on you.
You have to do what you do.
This day and age you better love who loves you.
But to procure a secure spot in my heart
You've got to be dark.
It's through and for the love of black women
That I'm livin'
And only black women that I've given
My mind, body, soul and heart
Because black people, we ain't never had much
And right now we are all we've got;
And if we cultivate that seed
Maybe we are all we need.
But I can only speak for me
And in life I can only play my part.
And you can measure the purity
Of these statements against the feather of ma'at
And the scales will not teeter-tot
And I will not betray your heart
Because from this day until the last that I've got
God know I love 'em dark.
God bless you black women.

The Sermon

After the verdict Saturday night, which saw george zimmerman exonerated of any wrong doing in the murder of Trayvon Martin, I went to church on Sunday morning waiting and wanting to hear… something. My emotions were strained; my eyes were brimming with tears of anger; my thoughts were set on seeking out true justice. In my mind I could hear the firebrand speeches of Dr. Martin Luther King Jr. and Malcolm X. I could clearly recall these recordings that called a community in turmoil into action; speeches that inspired men and women to endure the threat of dogs, hoses and batons for the betterment of the black community as a whole. Instead of the righteous indignation and call to organize, protest and fight that I expected… I was instead told to vote. I was told to stay calm. I was told that if one black boy goes to college because of this then Trayvon didn't die in vain. Although as far as zimmerman knew Trayvon could have very well been a calm black boy in college that had recently voted.

In the face of the ever rising toll of young black people senselessly murdered and what appears to be no solutions to stopping or stemming this troublesome tide, the words from the pulpit to vote, to be calm and to carry on felt hollow. They rattled and fell flat like the first nickel dropped into an empty piggy bank. Be calm and carry on felt like words stolen from British placards, like words being mailed in from the "What you tell black people after a tragedy," book of sermons. It felt like some ancient overseer was just over the pastor's shoulder whispering into his ear "Now tell 'em to be calm… now tell 'em to quietly carry on… now tell 'em to pick more cotton." I left feeling as frustrated and empty as I did when I arrived… and I was $20 poorer. So I decided to write something. I'm not a preacher. I'm a man who reads the bible but I wouldn't call myself a biblical scholar by any stretch of the imagination but if you have the time and inclination sit with me as I deliver a sermon more in the vein of what I expected to hear.

116

Good day, I want to start by saying if you're mad about the verdict in the Trayvon Martin case know that your anger is justified; know that you're not crazy; know that you're not playing the "race card" (as if this is some game); know that his MURDER was racially motivated; know that the justice system in the country is broken and know that I and millions of others are mad right alongside you!

I type these words as I listen to my 7 year old nephew play in the other room. I type these words knowing that my sister, and countless other black women have tears in their eyes and fear in their hearts knowing that their sons and daughters have to grow up in a nation where they can be murdered and the killer not be charged with ANYTHING; in a nation where you have to raise a national outcry just to have the most rudimentary of criminal investigations started; in a nation where in the face of overwhelming evidence of guilt you will be forced to sit and watch the killer of your child smile, wave, be given his gun back and walk free! I type these words after listening to white people call into WSB talk radio and say "I'm tired of black people and all their complaining! It's over, zimmerman is not guilty, get over it!" And if you listen closely and carefully to the vitriol in their voices you'll hear that what they're really saying is "Slavery is over, get over it!" "The lynchings are over, get over it!" "Jim Crow is over, get over it," "COINTELPRO is over, get over it," "The flooding of your communities with crack is over, get over it!" "Trayvon is dead! Get over it!" "The next insane injustice we will visit upon you will happen soon, but as soon as it's over… get over it!" I type these words knowing that some people think that having a black President somehow magically makes all racial injustice go away but understand that there is no rabbit in that hat; those thoughts are all sleight of hand and failing illusions. I type these words with fire in my veins, acid on my tongue and a heavy heart.

117

I know what happened to Trayvon Martin. I've heard zimmerman's 911 call. I've heard Rachel Jeantel's testimony. I've watched recreations of that fateful evening and having the sense God gave me I can paint a reasonable picture of the events. Let me summarize: Trayvon Martin PURCHASED some candy and a tea and was walking back to his father's residence. george zimmerman racially profiled Trayvon, called the police, was told to stand down and ignored that order. zimmerman followed Martin with a pistol. zimmerman never identified himself in any way to Trayvon and a confrontation ensued. Armed, adult, MMA trained zimmerman killed unarmed, teenage Trayvon Martin in cold blood. zimmerman was initially not charged with anything in conjunction with this murder. A national outcry saw him indicted and a lengthy trial saw justice not served and zimmerman freed.

We all collectively experienced the tragedy of this injustice and it sits like a stone in our hearts. I have personally shed tears and sat dumbfounded by the clear implications of zimmerman's acquittal. I KNOW what happened to Trayvon. The question I have now is … what happened to us? What happened to black people?

I began reading the story of Lazarus after church on Sunday and let me share a few verses from one of the most famous stories of the bible:

John 11:1-3
Now a man named Lazarus was sick. He was from Bethany, the village of Mary and her sister Martha. 2 (This Mary, whose brother Lazarus now lay sick, was the same one who poured perfume on the Lord and wiped his feet with her hair.) 3 So the sisters sent word to Jesus, "Lord, the one you love is sick."
John 11: 6-7
6 So when he heard that Lazarus was sick, he stayed where he was two more days, 7 and then he said to his disciples, "Let us go back to Judea."

118

John 11: 17

17 On his arrival, Jesus found that Lazarus had already been in the tomb for four days.

John 11:21

21 "Lord," Martha said to Jesus, "if you had been here, my brother would not have died.

John 11:32

32 When Mary reached the place where Jesus was and saw him, she fell at his feet and said, "Lord, if you had been here, my brother would not have died."

John 11:40-43

Then Jesus said, "Did I not tell you that if you believe, you will see the glory of God?" 41 So they took away the stone. Then Jesus looked up and said, "Father, I thank you that you have heard me. 42 I knew that you always hear me, but I said this for the benefit of the people standing here, that they may believe that you sent me."43 When he had said this, Jesus called in a loud voice, "Lazarus, come out!" 44 The dead man came out, his hands and feet wrapped with strips of linen, and a cloth around his face.

We were all taught the story of Lazarus in Sunday school. We all know that Lazarus died and that Jesus raised Lazarus from the dead. The name Lazarus itself means, "God is my help" and has become synonymous with renewal, rebirth and resurrection.

Jesus often taught in parables and in analogies so let us explore how the story of Lazarus might not just be a story that we all committed rote to memory but may be synonymous with our current situation.

In today's context let's look at Lazarus and let's look at ourselves.

What we know from the story is that Lazarus was not well, he had fallen ill after what we could assume was a time of good health. Lazarus had people in his life that loved him and when he fell ill sent word to Jesus their spiritual leader that "The one you love is sick." That also lets us know that Lazarus was not unknown to his spiritual leader and that the leader, Jesus, loved Lazarus.

Lazarus was failed by his leadership and did indeed die. When Jesus finally showed up the people who loved Lazarus said "if you'd have been here my brother wouldn't have died." The people had clearly lost their faith in their leadership. Their leadership then showed them that when all hope is lost and when properly led and motivated amazing things are possible. Lazarus was raised from the dead.

So in these modern days and times... who is Lazarus?
Let's imagine Lazarus as the African American community as a whole; and let's cast Jesus as the modern day church.

African Americans are a people who in this nation were birthed through the fire of forced servitude, of iron shackles, of the lash, of violent rape and of the forced division of their families. We did not enter this nation on Mayflowers, Ninas, Pintas or Santamarias. We did not arrive in comfortable cabins or on the deck of ships smiling and waving at the growing land mass in the distance. No, we found permanent and compulsory footing in America on Amistads, Coras, Henrietta Maries and Braunfischs. We were birthed as African Americans in the rancid bellies of ships running molasses, rum and slave labor between Europe, Africa and the (now) United States. Our men were forced to their knees in supplication, our women forced on their backs in subjugation AND YET AND STILL we somehow managed to make it to our feet and find ourselves as a community navigating these rough waters toward less turbulent but certainly not tranquil seas. We in time found a sense of identity in our African American duality, a sense of pride through our struggle, we banded together to fight injustice and we were well on our way to some sense of wholeness if not completeness. We put our Orishas and Loas on the shelf along the way and picked up instead the spiritual leadership of our oppressors, Christianity as represented by the church. We knew the church and the church knew us. We loved the church… and felt that the church loved us.

After shaking off our manacles and straightening our scarred backs we found that we were having growing pains and those who'd rather not see us grow mainly inflicted those pains. Those who stood in our sunlight and only cast shadow were causing our pains. Those that stood on our shoulders and screamed "pull yourself up by your bootstraps," were stunting our growth. In the face of dogs, hoses, poll taxes, bullets, lynchings, batons, jail cells and shallow graves we stood resolute and undeterred. Our movement and mantra was ever forward and amongst ourselves and as a people things seemed to be headed in the right direction. We didn't have what we wanted but we knew what we needed and we began to ask for it, to march for it, to sit-in for it, to boycott for it and to fight for it!

Then we fell ill. To say we fell ill is actually incorrect. It seems that in truth illness was forced upon us. We were a healthy body of dreamers, fighters and believers when our heart was stopped (Dr. Martin Luther King Jr. 1968, Memphis, TN), our mind was removed (Malcolm X, 1965, New York City) and our spirit exorcised (Medgar Evars, 1963, Jackson, MS). The church in its many forms had over time become the source of our strength and wellness and so we turned to the church and said, "Help! The one you love is sick!"

Our spiritual leadership failed us. They picked the wrong battles and preached messages about sole, endless prosperity instead of the soul's

121

endless posterity. They took up the interests of corporations instead of working toward the corporate interest of the people. Did all do this? No. There were some like John the Baptist in the wilderness shouting the truth. Those that garnered the most attention however, that were given national stages, worldwide televised broadcasts, audiences with presidents and dignitaries they fostered the most base and destructive of ideals. They built mansions and mega churches, they flew private jets and drove Bentley's ... and they left us to die as they looked down from alabaster towers built on our trust and with our money.

And die we did, in Chicago, in New York, in Ohio, in Georgia, in Sanford, FL. We died while supporting trends that whispered of our demise. We died while watching programs that showed us plainly the path to our ruin. We died while listening to music that trumpeted our death from speakers that could be heard for miles. We became a people holding both an iPhone and a pistol to our heads, a people with one foot in the club and the other in a grave. We have fallen ill and in many ways we have been allowed, by those who call themselves our leaders, to die.

But if the parable holds true we don't have to stay dead! We can find life! We can be called back to life! We can have our faith in our leadership restored. We can shake off this death that we have put on so easily, so readily and we can once again begin moving toward the good of our community. We, the black community still have time to become Lazarus from the grave but we must begin now! We must begin now to take the reins and steer ourselves back toward the path of greatness. We must know that no one else is going to do it for us! We must look out for, care for, educate, trust and believe in ourselves! If we do not then know that the stone in our hearts will not roll away and we will not emerge renewed from this time of death and injustice. The choice is ours and in truth there is no choice!

Let us once again revisit the story of Lazarus and cast it in another light. Let us consider for a moment that the black community is Jesus and Lazarus represents our children, our beautiful brown babies. Our children are trying to negotiate this wilderness of glorified prison culture and an ever growing prison industrial complex; this wilderness of being over medicated and under educated; this wilderness of being inundated with media that promotes everything from misogyny to masochism. Maybe Lazarus represents these children whose mothers scream to the black community "Help! The one you love is sick."

And how have our children become so ill? They have been sickened by being labeled a threat just for being who they are! They have been sickened by being black children that are perceived as being more of a threat holding a can of soda, than a white man is holding a loaded gun! They have been sickened by being black children that have been more scandalized for wearing hoodies to cross the street than white men have been for wearing hoods to burn crosses in yards! They have been sickened by watching a professional football player that killed dogs go to jail for two years while the murderer of a young black man walks free! They have been sickened by watching another professional football player that shot HIMSELF go to jail for two years while the murderer of a young black man walks free! They are sickened by the two judicial systems in America, the one for minorities and the one for whites! They are sick of it all and we should be too!

But many in the community are so busy watching *Basketball Wives* or working 60 hour work weeks or trying to keep up appearances that they're too tired to be sickened; too distracted to be sickened or too sick themselves to be able to aid in the saving of these precious babies.

But if the parable holds true, all it will take is for the community to show up and to call our children's names for them to wake up, for them to live again! All it will take is for the community to take an interest, to come together as one and roll away the stone that is separating us from our young ones! We can breathe life into a dying situation but it's going to take some focus, time and effort. It's going to take some understanding. It's going to take meeting people where they are and bringing them to where they should be. The road from death to life is not an easy one but it is a journey we must take if we are to have any hope of a future that sees our babies healthy and whole.

Whether Lazarus represents the black community, our kids or ourselves, he receives what so many of us need; he receives what zimmerman's acquittal should have been to us, what the gutting of the Voting Rights Act should have been to us, what the media ignoring the epidemic of young black death in Chicago should be to us, what Marissa Alexander's incarceration should be to us; Lazarus receives a wake up call and after this weekend, in the black community all eyes should be open.

-Amen-

Dread Scott [A Haiku / A Reaction to the Murder of Walter Scott]

How scared are they of
Us that they must still handcuff
Us, as we lay dead.

I'm going to name my son CVS
Lest they forget that he is something of value.
A child who they shouldn't pretend to forfend
But actually protect!

Lest they forget
To say his real name!
That he is beautiful, unusual and rare
And not their Shanequa Gay Fair Game, usual suspect.

Lest they forget that
When they had the uprising in Maryland,
Because blacks and whites
Dressed in blue killed Gray red handed; while justice, not surprising,
Was left debating rights and splitting hairs again.
Justice was stuck in its train of thought, shells and suits.
All hell broke loose and it moved its scales and caboose as slow as a
terrapin.

Until the next thing you know tempers flared
And then
A flare pierced the air
And when
That CVS caught fire
It was all that CNN was airing then!

They called it an act of terror and
It's where all their cameras and their caring went.
Gray matters slipped their minds
And corporate interests is where it went.
And since legally corporations are people without pulse or context;

126

And since black people have deceivingly gone from sharecroppers
To commodities for shareholders in the prison industrial complex;
All of this suggests
That I shouldn't name my son Amadou or Trayvon or Tamir.
No names from the triangle trade or trail of tears.
No names of color.
It's clear, in the U.S.
If I wish for him to be blessed with success and clout
And not be shot in the chest with his hands up
And be left in the street to bleed out
 I MUST name him CVS.

Lest they forget that he is important
And not just when in court and
In jumpsuits;
Or in war and
On the front line in front of troops.

Lest they forget that he is loved.
He is not a thug dealing drugs chasing after fast cash.
He is not a soul out of control dying to be your next hashtag;
Dying to be your next rest in peace t-shirt;
Dying to be your next early morning Instagram like or
Late night Google site keyword search.
No!

And I know there's no debating,
If I wanted him to start out with hate and
End up with Vanity, fanfare, respect;
An overnight sensation
With a twitter account that crashes the Internet;
I could absolutely name him Caitlin.

Or no lyin' maine (lion mane)
If I wanted him to maintain
The pride of his people;
To have the whole world cry
When he dies and still be considered regal;
I should definitely name him Cecil.

Or in this arena
As it stands
If I wanted white America
To view him as, treat him like and call him a man;
I should name him Serena.

If I want him to drown in his sorrows with no prevention;
To be abandoned in his residence by his President
With no government help or intervention;
I should name him Katrina

Or if I want him to be good for nothing, name him FEMA.

I definitely can't name him Baptist Church.
They'll co-op his vote, post-op his hope
And undermine his history, time and worth.
Even worse,
Is that he can be under attack for weeks;
A hot bed set afire by the ire of confederate flags and white sheets.
He can be ablaze, ignored for days
And when the media finally chooses to speak
They'll say it was an act of God;
Not even on TV but late evening
Via a Facebook post and a tweet.

Naming him Martin King will get him blasted within a week.

Naming him Fred Hampton will get him assassinated in his sleep.
Naming him Renisha McBride will get him shot while seeking help;
and hell
Naming him Sandra Bland will get him killed for improper signal,
alone in a cell.

Swisher sweets, reaching for your wallet, toy guns,
Walking home in the street, the midnight moon, the noonday sun;
These are the spaces, places and reasons
They give for killing our Oshuns and Oguns,
Yemayas, Obatalas, our daughters and our sons.

Oh but a CVS?
A CVS they will respect, serve and protect
With their last breath and the National Guard;
With tanks, riots gear masks, tear gas,
Guns, prayers and offer thanks to God!

Harm a CVS and they will pass new laws.
Raise your hand to a CVS and find yourself behind bars.
So I offer a wink, a nod and Kanye shrug when
I say I'm going to name my son CVS
Lest the U.S. forgets…
That I love him.

Ain't Worried About Nothing

Tuesday July 16th 2013 | 7:00 p.m. Atlanta, Georgia | Five Points Station | Southbound Platform:

I was headed home after spending the greater part of my day at Marlee's Coffeehouse on Decatur St. working on a new play. Marlee's is a nice quaint black owned coffee house that hosts a weekly open mic on Tuesday nights AND it's right beside the King Memorial MARTA station (I'm a sucker for convenience and a proponent of supporting black business). I chatted up Tawny Powell and Mistafunn for a bit then headed out before the open mic started. I had more work to do and an open mic was not going to help me get it done. I hopped the west bound train at MLK where I immediately encountered a woman with the word "Crazy" tattooed on one arm and "Bitch" tattooed on the other; and I thought to myself after a night of malt liquor, lemon pepper wangs in a Styrofoam container, a Tyler Perry movie and aggressive sex where everyone involved is called a b!tch at least once; when you wake up the next morning only to find a knife sticking out of your bicep and your penis super glued to your thigh, you can't say you weren't warned. I then thought, wouldn't it be great though if EVERYONE came with such truthful labels? You meet a guy and his left leg is tattooed with the word "Deadbeat" and the right "Dad." You meet a woman and her left shoulder reads "I Can't" and her right spells out "Cook." You encounter a man and tattooed about his six pack a la Tupac are the words "Bad" and "Credit." When I met my ex-wife if she'd have had the words "I Will" tattooed over her top lip and "Leave You" tattooed beneath the lower it may have trumped the "I do" that would escape from between them later. Wouldn't that make life and dating much more upfront and far easier? Dam speed dating! This would turn dating into RIF (Reading is Fundamental). At Mardi Gras I'll throw you some beads if you show me your tats!

I rode the train from King Memorial to Five Points Station and headed over to the southbound platform, which would take me to my final destination College Park Station. As I was standing on the Platform I noticed two guys waiting for the southbound train. They were on opposite southbound platforms separated by the expanse that housed the train tracks. One guy had on a t-shirt that read "Angry Birds" with what appeared to be an illustration of three kilos of cocaine with frowny faces drawn on them, and a pair of sagging jeans. His arms were heavily tattooed. Many of the tattoos seemed to read "RIP_____" (fill in the blank). He was a walking monument to lives lost too soon; a mobile memorial made of flesh. While speaking he would gesture wildly with his right hand while his left was tasked with the herculean effort of keeping his pants from falling to his ankles … they were already to his knees it seemed. Across from him was a guy that, right or wrong, most people would stereotype as a criminal at first glance. He had baby dreads, a gold grill, black tears tattooed beside his right eye, a cross tattooed in the center of his forehead, an ampersand tattooed on his right cheek, a Chinese letter tattooed on his left cheek and other random symbols emblazoned on his chin. I felt like all of the tattoos were saying something very abstract, uniform and amazingly hood in their various languages and symbolic representations. It was like he had a ghetto Rosetta Stone tattooed on his face. He was wearing what appeared to be three t-shirts (on a very warm day), sagging Dickies pants and a pair of Air Force Ones. If this was *The First 48* he'd have been picked up as a person of interest within the first 24. But looking like what society thinks a criminal must look like is not a crime in and of itself. Besides how many men have stolen billions in Brooks Brothers suits? How many politicians have lied and stolen from their constituency while smiling their perfectly capped teeth smile? Maybe the definition of what a criminal looks like should be redefined.

Across the tracks on opposing southbound platforms, Walking Memorial and Rosetta Face carried on a conversation that was chock

131

full of "Got damns" and "Sh!!!!ts." They were both toeing the far edge of the yellow line that denotes the "do not cross" barrier; the barrier that is supposed to keep pedestrians from getting too close to the approaching train. As they conversed back and forth a Caucasian police officer with a buzz cut and a clear penchant for aggressively chewing gum appeared out of nowhere as if conjured from some Fruitvale Station boogeyman house of horrors and began walking down the platform. Every eye on the platform fell on the officer. We were just four days removed from the Trayvon Martin miscarriage of justice and all uniformed authority figures were being met with hard stares, balled fists, clenched jaws and tight lips. Both platforms fell eerily silent save the two gentlemen still speaking, oblivious to the officer's entrance and approach stage left.

Rosetta Face was standing so close to the "do not cross" line of demarcation that the only reasonable way to pass him would be to walk behind him and there was enough room behind him to park a train, thus making passing behind him an easy and attractive alternative to trying to squeeze in front. The Caucasian officer, however, slowly approached and slowly walked through the narrow space in front of Rosetta Face. He passed so closely it seemed at one point their faces would meet nose to nose. The officer then proceeded to walk around him in a tight circle before walking off. It was almost like a shark circling his prey or a buzzard circling what he assumed was an already dead carcass. An audible buzz began on both platforms and an older gentleman on the opposite platform screamed over "What the f#ck was that? WHAT THE F#CK WAS THAT!?" This gentleman's question, that simultaneously was and was not rhetorical, helped others to find their voices. A woman beside me shouted "What the f#ck!?" Others rumbled and stirred. An ancient voice tired of being mistreated, tired of being abused, tired of turning the other cheek began to birth its way from their throats and rise to the surface. Then Rosetta Face spoke and said "He must have thought I had some Skittles in my pocket or

132

something." This did not remove the palpable tension in the air but it did serve to make it so that your jaw could be tight and you could chuckle a bit at the same damn time. Rosetta Face continued "Oh and don't let me have an iced tea, you know Skittles AND an iced tea is like a weapon of mass destruction out this b!tch!" That statement elicited a few full out laughs and a couple of "I know that's rights" from onlookers; and now he had both platforms' full attention. Knowing he had the crowd he raised his voice and said, "They want me to do something stupid! They want me to pop off! They want me to go to jail today but 'N!@@a I ain't worried about nothing, n!@@a I ain't worried about nothing…'" then both platforms joined in with "Ehhhhh ain't worried about nothing!" echoing the French Montana anthem. It was weird, but in that moment I felt like I completely understood why dudes in the hood felt that song so strongly in their spirit. Up until that VERY moment I'd thought of French Montana's "Ain't Worried About Nothin" as just another in a long line of "disposable, ring-tone, you'll be embarrassed that you liked that in five years" songs. But in a world where if you're black, poor, marginalized, profiled and have so much to worry about, up to and including your life, a song that flies in the face of that struggle, that becomes what Nam Myoho Renge Kyo is to Buddhist, what Hare Krishna is to followers of Krishna, what steady, constant and ecstatic rotation is to a whirling dervish, has to seem like a mantra and message for the ages. They must feel like words that you can say and just get mindlessly lost in their recitation. They must seem like words that, while you're saying them, put you in a place beyond the reach of the long arm of the law, beyond lady justice's selective blindness, beyond any worry. I stood on that platform and found myself bouncing, nodding my head and chanting along with the group "Ni@@a I ain't worried about nothing!" And I felt good.

Rosetta Face spoke again "You see! All that marching and singing We Shall Overcome is dead! What's coming next is fists upside m#th#f#kas heads!" Both platforms looked at him and nodded. "They just don't know! Trayvon done started some $#!T! Letting zimmerman go done started some $#!T! They just don't know Bruh!" Both platforms looked at him and nodded. Rosetta Face had begun his sermon on the mount, his declaration of independence, his emancipation proclamation and he'd found a congregation eager for the word. He continued, "Watch bruh! Watch and see if what I tell you ain't truth. That asking $#!T is done… we taking!" A few voices rose up with "Yeahs!" and a few applause even sounded out as the College Park bound train rolled into the station.

Everyone boarded and there was a visceral energy flowing through the occupants of the train. Folks looked each other in the eye and nodded like, "You feel me?" "You heard?" and I met their gaze with "Ehhh ain't worried about nothing," echoing through my mind.

CHAPTER SIX

"To be nobody but yourself in a world that's doing its best to make you somebody else, is to fight the hardest battle you are ever going to fight. Never stop fighting."-E.E. Cumming

Scotch whisky (often referred to simply as "Scotch") is malt whisky or grain whisky made in Scotland. All Scotch whisky was originally made from malt barley. Commercial distilleries began introducing whisky made from wheat and rye in the late eighteenth century.

"First thing I remember was asking papa, why, / For there were many things I didn't know. / And daddy always smiled and took me by the hand, / Saying, someday you'll understand," - Credence Clearwater Revival

<u>Pop Loves Scotch</u>

Pop loves scotch.
I wasn't absolutely sure if pop loved mom
But I was absolutely sure that pop, he loved scotch.
One time pop, scotch and a snub nosed .32 cleared three blocks
And that was done strictly for his love of scotch.
But pop hated drug dealers
And pop hated wife beaters
Although he was known to sell scotch to his friends
And sometimes with mom he got a little free with his hands
And with tears in his eyes
He'd look into her tear stained eyes
And he'd apologize.
Nevermore like the Raven he would quote
So drug dealer, wife beater
To a lesser extent he was both
But pop just loved scotch.
He always had a taste of Cutty Sark or 100 Pipers with him
And if he got fifty of those pipers in his system
Then you could not miss him.
He was at the same time charming and alarming
So women could not resist him.

And his thoughts on marriage were in passing

And not everlasting

So he would not resist them.

My father was having a love affair with scotch.

I remember one time my brother drug sick and high as a kite

With pop picked a fight.

It was at pop's place

That he slapped pop in the face

And that was all she wrote.

Pop screamed, "Are you crazy boy!"

He came out of his lazy boy like a d@mn lighting bolt.

Now pop and bro both threw and took plenty

But bro took too many.

Anguished and vanquished down went the first son

Then pop spent on me the second seed

And said, "Do you want some!"

"Hell no," I replied

And handed his @ss a glass

Of scotch on the double

Because pop loved scotch

And lord knows I didn't want any trouble.

With age came wisdom and an irregular heart rhythm.

Now pop's an old cat

And even he would true that.

He worked hard and played hard

But on your body and soul

It'll take a toll when you do that.

And few cats that he knew

That were known to do what he do

Have lived as long as he has.

Many have passed.

And sometimes I have to question pop's health some.

His health will have the prodigal son dialing 911

Saying hurry up because Isaac needs help with Abraham.
And all those days of ham,
Cigarettes and liquor living like a heathen
Has had his body at odds but now his body's getting even.
Late one night
Pop looked at me and said, "Son I ain't lived right.
I did the best I could do with what I had and what I knew.
Facing the same situations you'd probably do the same things too."
Then spasm he went into
Clutching at his chest
But he couldn't catch his breath.
He was caught by the heart cops
And put under cardiac arrest.
I rushed him to the hospital where they were pushing on his chest.
They gave him 2cc's of breathe pop breathe
And told me to step into the hall while he got a little rest.
The doctor gave a sigh and then
Pulled down his wire rims
And said, "The problem with your pop
Is that your pop's got problems.
Emphysema, hypertension
Not to mention his dedication
To prescription medication trying to solve them.
You see the pills your pop's been popping
Would be helping a lot
But after pill popping
Your pop's scoffing down scotch."
I looked the doctor dead into his eyes
And said, "Look I've advised
Pop several times
Of the several lines he's crossed."
You see the cost, he's lost
Money, health and wife

But pop loves scotch more than pop loves life.
He will not go gentle into that good night!
He will rage, rage against the dying of the light!
Against the grim reaper clash while standing on the brink
And he will whip the reaper's @ss if he makes him spill his drink!
From my first to my last I've got love for pop.
I remember being in the fifth grade and getting out of my last class
And running home quick, fast,
Just to watch pop watch TV.
He was hugging and kissing a glass filled to the top.
I remember wishing pop loved me, as much as pop loves scotch
… because pop loves scotch.

When you ask a room full of children what they want to be when they grow up the answers are as varied as the children themselves. Girls, regardless of race and economic background, often want to be images from Disney films and tales told to them as they nod off into restful slumber. They want to be sleeping beauties saved by white men on white horses, whisked off to White Castles (not the fast food restaurant, no one wants to be whisked there) and awoken with magical kisses. They want the fantasy they've been promised so earnestly as, now I lay me down to sleep. Other little girls with more forward thinking mothers; mothers that saw their adult lives poisoned by the Disney-fication of their life expectations; mothers that kissed frogs that never proved to be more than just horned toads. These mothers pull their daughters heads from the clouds and out of fairytales. At a very early age they inspire their daughters to think outside of all preconceived and conventional boxes, to once and for all shatter all glass ceilings and slippers. These girls often grow up wanting to be agents of change. So today little girls not only dream of being princesses they also aspire toward the reality of one day being heads of state, Presidents.

Boys with their testosterone bubbling just below the surface, their fathers with dreams deferred living vicariously through their not even fully formed first steps; with a football placed in their crib as a chew toy; with a toy gun placed in the hand opposite their rattle often imagine themselves as more aggressive things when they grow up. They see themselves as astronauts, police officers, members of the X-Men, firefighters, sports stars and yes... heads of state, Presidents.

This is before many parents start to feed their kids a steady diet of full servings of harsh realities alongside their grilled cheese sandwiches and Kool Aid. This is before "Go to college and get a good job." This is before "What are you going to do with a degree in that?" This is before

"Forget what makes you happy, think about what makes you money." This is before kids are read the stats and quoted the odds. This is before dreams go from incredible to inane; from impossible to mundane. This is when the mantra is still, "You can be anything you want to be" and it is Nam Myoho Renge Kyo-ed in their ears daily.

Wednesday 12/10/13 4:30 p.m.
I pick up my nephew Joshua at Imhotep Academy, a school in downtown Atlanta, where the minds of young African American students are nurtured, refined and molded into thinking machines that are socially conscious, aware of their history, steeped in the present and pointed toward a successful future. Joshua is everything a seven year old boy is supposed to be, he's smart, he's curious, he's athletic, he's rambunctious, he... thinks he knows EVERYTHING. I'm sure he wonders how it is possible that in his mere seven years of living on this earth he's been able to solve ALL of the great mysteries that so many grown ups have had a lifetime to ponder and decipher. I'm sure he wonders this despite the fact that tying his own shoelaces still gives him fits some days. I hop out of the car and walk to the school's gym that serves as a launching pad for children that have counted down to the end of the school day and are now primed and ready to rocket their way into their parent's arms and towards home.

Joshua: Uncle Jon!
Me: Joshua!
Joshua: Uncle Jon!
Me: Joshua!
Joshua: Ok... enough of that. I didn't know you were picking me up.
Me: The truth of it is self-evident.
Joshua: What does that mean?
Me: I'm clearly here to pick you up. Let's go.

On our way toward leaving Joshua playfully jostles a few male friends, laughs and runs away from a girl that has proven, even at this early stage in life, too amorous for his tastes. He grabs his book bag, waves a few final goodbyes and we exit the gym toward the car.

Me: So what do you want for dinner?
Joshua: A turkey burger from Zestos!!
Me: Ok... I'll go to the one near the house, the one in Forest Park.

We drive and enjoy a conversation about every possible power and ability of Superman and The Green Lantern. I'm informed that The Green Arrow in DC comics is OKAY but Hawkeye in Marvel comics is FAR superior. Joshua is baffled as to why Wonder Woman can fly AND has an invisible plane. He then goes on to take me on a frame-by-frame explanation of the movie *Man of Steel*; even though I've seen the movie he's convinced that his insight into the film must be known and shared. I don't argue. I don't pummel him with the, "Be quiet!" that my father kept always on the tip of his tongue. I don't place in front of his free thought association conversation the children are to be seen and not heard placards of old. I let him talk. I let him laugh. I let him think. I ask him questions. I challenge his reasoning. He answers my challenges. I let him be.

We pull into the Forest Park, Georgia Zestos and order two turkey burger combos. As we wait a man standing roughly five foot, eight inches and weighing what has to be four hundred pounds lumbers in after having just pried himself from the cab of a Peterbilt eighteen wheeler. He orders what sounds like a little bit of everything then sits on the bench adjacent to me and Joshua.

Trucker: How y'all doing?
Me: We're good and you?

Trucker: I'm good. Starving! I've got a hollow 'round about here ... (He rubs his protruding stomach that appears to have not been hollow in quiet some time) that needs filling! I ordered a little bit of everything!

I look at this man that is grossly overweight; I peruse the empty calories on the Zestos menu and realize he is probably also grossly malnourished. Overweight and malnourished. What irony.

Trucker: They don't have these in Jacksonville. I live down there with my girlfriend (there's a pause) ... she's black.

I say nothing.

Trucker: I think all people are the same you know! I can't wait to see her. When I bring her back up this way I'll have to bring her here.

I say nothing again but think to myself, you really know how to show a lady a good time.
The attendant behind the counter at Zestos that looks like Patsy Cline and Willie Nelson's long lost love child calls my order number, Joshua and I stand to retrieve our food and leave.

Me: Travel safely.
Trucker: (extends his hand) Thank you.

I shake his hand and notice his confederate flag embossed belt buckle. A black girlfriend and a confederate flag embossed belt buckle. What irony.

Joshua and I jump in the car and begin to head home. I'm driving in a group of cars herded together on their way up Forest Parkway when I spot an officer's vehicle just ahead. He's parked in the median his truck perched like a coyote surveying a gathering of approaching goats. The

143

vehicles traveling in the pack I'm in are all going about the same speed. No one is pulling away and I'm near the rear. I see the coyote pull out and get fast on our trail. I think to myself he's either pulling ALL of us over or NONE of us because we're all going about the same speed. The coyote falls in behind me. I think to myself, there is no way he's pulling me over. I'm at the rear of this pack; clearly the cars in front of me are traveling just as fast if not faster than I am. To pull me over would be … absurd. His lights and siren come on. The rest of the cars bolt leaving me to be the one devoured by the coyote, the apparent weakest of the pack. I pull over to the right and go through the check list drilled into all black boys by their fathers at the age of 15: #1 Pull over (check): #2 Turn off the vehicle (check): #3 Put your hands on the steering wheel or hang them out of the window (I always opt for the steering wheel. check): #4 Make no sudden moves (check). #5 Know your rights (check). Checklist complete. I'm sitting perfectly still with my hands on the steering wheel, my heart in my throat and my palms beginning to perspire. I have done nothing wrong that I know of yet and still this is my automatic reaction when a police car pulls in behind me, when the blue lights come on, when the siren sounds. Nervousness, angst... fear. I wait for the officer. A coyote howls somewhere in the back of my mind.

The man that knocks on my window looks to be barely a man. The officer appears to be just north of twenty years old the remnants of teenage acne still apparent on his now clearing skin. His gun weighs awkwardly on his hip. His gun belt leans with the weight of his pistol spaghetti western style, Clint Eastwood Fist Full of Dollars style. His bullet proof vest swallows the whole of him. He looks like someone who hasn't been told that Halloween has passed, a kid playing dress up. I gesture toward the car's key. He nods. I turn the key, roll the window down and return my hands to the steering wheel. Joshua says nothing.

Officer: Do you know why I pulled you over?

Me: I have no idea.

Officer: Do you know what the speed limit is on Forest Parkway?

Me: It's 40.

Officer: How fast do you think you were traveling?

This road side pop quiz final jeopardy $#!T always infuriates me. I didn't bring a number two pencil. I didn't study the materials the night before. I'm ill prepared for this GMAT (Georgia M#thaf##in Auto Test). Plus you wouldn't care for the actual answers floating through my head.

Me: 45, 50 at the most. The same speed as the REST of the cars.

Officer: License and proof of insurance.

Me: (loudly, slowly and clearly) I'm reaching into my pocket to get my wallet.

Officer: Okay.

Me: I'm going to ask you to calibrate your radar gun while you run my information.

Officer: (smiling a broad and somewhat menacing smile) ... Absolutely.

I hear a coyote howl in the back of my mind.

I hand over the materials. I watch him scurry back to his vehicle seemingly salivating over the fresh kill in his grasp. I roll up the window and continue talking Ironman and Black Widow with Joshua. The officer returns and stands near my rear bumper with his hand resting ominously near his gun.

Officer: I'm going to need you to step out of the vehicle!

A police officer shouting for you to step out of the vehicle is NEVER good news. It's never, "You're dressed real sharp today sir! Step out of the vehicle and lets discuss your haberdasher." It's never, "You know what I've had a rough day, step out of the vehicle and give me a hug." It's certainly never, "I re-calibrated my radar gun and you were right, step out of the vehicle and tase me for the b#llsh!t I'm on." I step out of the vehicle and slowly join the officer near the vehicle's rear bumper.

Officer: The system shows that your license is suspended.
Me: It was, but I paid all of the money to have it re-instated. I have the paper work in my bag.
Officer: Okay, let me see it.

Here is where I realize I have my red backpack and not my blue satchel bag... and the paper work is in the blue bag.

Me: You know what officer... what's your name officer?
Officer: Farrell.
Me: Like Will Ferrell?
Officer: Yeah but spelled with an "A," it's F -"A"-r-r-e-l-l.
Me: I see. Officer Farrell the paper work is actually in my other bag. My sister lives twenty minutes away. The young man in the car with me is my nephew. I can have her here in twenty minutes with the paper work.
Officer: (Looks at me. Looks at the car. Looks at Joshua)... okay... but I'm going to have to cuff you and put you in my truck.
Me: (Pointing at the car) But my nephew is the car!?
Officer: Call your sister, put her on the phone with your nephew, turn on the heat for him, then I WILL cuff you and put you in the truck.

The thoughts and emotions I'm faced with in this moment are almost indescribable. I'm angry. I'm being told to leave my seven-year-old nephew alone in a car on the side of the road in Georgia. I'm hurt. I'm being told that I'll be handcuffed in front of my seven-year-old nephew. I'm worried. I'm being told that I'm going to be put in the back of a police vehicle, a space that has served as the final resting place for more minorities than we know or speak of; a space that some have walked willfully into only to emerge innocently from a jail cell 10 years later. An apology from the warden, mayor and governor can never give them back the years they've lost.

I lean into the car to raise my sister on the phone and turn on the heat. My nephew is already in tears.

Joshua: What's going on Uncle Jon!
Me: It's okay Josh. I'm okay and you're okay. I'm going to get your mom on the phone she's going to talk to you while I sit back in the car with the police officer.
Joshua: Can I sit with you!?
Me: No... you're okay though. You're a big boy. I'll be in the car right behind you. I can see you. You're okay.
Joshua: ... Uncle Jon ... is he going to kill you?

My heart breaks because I know that for him it has begun. I know that from this day forward every time a cop pulls in behind him his palms will sweat, his heart will race and he will wonder if he'll survive the experience. I know that even as a law abiding citizen he will live with a cigar box filled with bail beneath his bed just in case. I know that the stories he's heard lately on the news about Trayvon Martin, Kendrick Johnson and Renisha McBride are leaping off of the screen and playing out right before his eyes. I know that stories he doesn't know but must resonate on some unknown level with his soul, Oscar Grant, Timothy Stansbury, Amadou Diallo, Sean Bell and the countless others must be whispering in his ear. These are the truly grim cautionary tales that brothers whisper to their sons in way of warning. These are the dark yarns that we're told to get over, to forget, to forgive, to accept as part of the African American experience. I know that his fear is real, his

147

suspicions justified by history … and that there is nothing I can do in this moment to rectify or change that.

Joshua begins to cry and I tell him what I don't know for sure, I tell him everything is going to be okay. His mother, my sister answers the phone. I tell her the situation, tell her where I am, tell her to stay on the phone with Joshua and to bring the blue bag post haste. I turn on the heat, exit the car, I'm handcuffed and I hear Joshua go into hysterics. My already broken heart finds a way to break again.

In the back of the police vehicle I sit fuming. My exterior is calm, it's placid, it is the Pacific Ocean but inside it's 79 AD and I am Vesuvius. I know that my anger will not serve me in this situation. I also know that if I take emotionality out of it, Officer Farrell doesn't have to give me these twenty minutes. He could very easily have called another squad car, had my nephew taken to the police precinct to be picked up by my sister, had my car impounded and taken me to jail. Officer Farrell could have told me what other officers black and white have told countless people in my position in the past... tell it to the judge. I thank God for small and larger favors. Officer Farrell begins to speak.

Officer: The young man in the car is your nephew?
Me: He is. He's my sister's son.
Officer: I'm about to be an uncle soon.
Me: Do you have any kids of your own?
Officer: No.
Me: Then until you do having a nephew or niece will be one of the most rewarding experiences in your life.
Officer: Yeah. Me and my sister are close.
Me: So am I with mine.
Officer: … Did you really clear this up Mr. Goode?
Me: I did. The paperwork will show.

Officer: (Looks toward the car where Joshua is) I hope so (there's a long pause)... he'll probably never trust the police again.
Me: Probably not.
Officer: (shakes his head).

I'm in the squad car for roughly thirty minutes when my sister arrives. She hands the officer the bag and he in turn hands the bag to me. With cuffed wrists I retrieve the paper work and hand it to him. He peruses the receipts, the money order Xeroxes, the official city and county documents with their raised seals and stamped signatures. He thumbs through them all two or three times. He shakes his head. He gets out of the squad car and comes around the back to where I'm uncomfortably seated.

Officer: You're right Mr. Goode. Let me get those cuffs off you.

I lift my hands as if in prayer, as if receiving the holy sacrament, he inserts the key into one side and then the other and takes off the cuffs. I am Houdini unbound. In my head I can't help but think of all of the men and women that have not had my fortune in this situation, that didn't get those thirty minutes to prove innocence. Men and women that have found themselves in cells or in graves for infractions as, if not more, minor than mine. Officer Farrell apologizes but still gives me the speeding ticket. He tells me to go to DDS the next day and get everything ironed out so that I don't show up as having a suspended license in the system and I can in the future avoid "this." Part of me wants to explain the seemingly unavoidable nature of "this." I don't. I walk back to the car where my nephew and sister await. Joshua hugs my neck with tears still wet on his face.

Me: I'm okay man... okay.
Joshua: okay... Uncle Jon?
Me: Yes.

Joshua: I don't want to be a policeman anymore.

Me No?

Joshua: No! I would still be President... or Wolverine though.

As for Joshua and what he wants to do with his life all things are to him still possible... save one.

And somewhere in the back of my mind I hear a coyote howl.

"Most men lead lives of quiet desperation and go to the grave with the song still in them."— *Henry David Thoreau*

200 Million Clark Kents

I suppose there were about a billion boys in the Justice League.
I'm talking coast to coast, sea to shining sea.
A bunch of snotty nose kids in tattered jeans
And dirty tees.
They'd stand on their tip toes
Point their hands toward the sun
And at the top of their lungs
They'd scream "Up, up and away!"
And no matter how impossible or improbable it seemed
With a towel tied around their necks
Hanging just below their knees
And an "S" magic markered on their chests
They'd try to fly in their dungarees.
Yes!
They had the fire of youth in their eyes.
They swore they'd always tell the truth,
Save the damsel in distress
And the world from its demise.
Yes!
They had the kind of imagination
That innovation and creation demand.
They were all in the Justice League
And they all truly believed
They'd grow up one day to be a super man.

And 20 years later many sit
Dutiful,
Dressed to impress,

151

Everyday
In their cubicles…
Depressed.
Staring at screens
With youthful dreams
They'd never dare admit.
I confess
Out of a billion I've seen at least 200 million boys
No less,
That have become men and let
Time cover up the "S" on their chest.
Stressed
Because they've been forced to forget
That they are the sons of Jor-El;
That they are really Kal-El.
They forget that they had plans to be Superman.
And there they stand
On the north bound platform
Or stuck in the morning drive
Rushing off to their 9 to 5's
Thinking that's that for 'em.
These super men
Think the pin stripes on their suits
Are iron bars they can't bend.
As they sit at their desks
Filling out tax forms.
Faster than a speeding bullet and
Swift as the wind
They quickly discover
That the rat race is one not even Superman can win.
If their youth is looked back on
You'll see the heat of their visions have died behind their eyes.
The "S" on their chests is hidden behind designer ties.

Kids that had made decisions to saving lives
Now save tithes
To give to super villains
Who use God as their disguise.
What kind of Bizarro world is this?
Where we've all got it about as backward as Mxylplyx,
Where Superman grows to be Clark Kent;
A day trader watching Oprah
That trades in his cape for a Rover.
He stays late, he works over
And pins all of his hopes to bank and post-it-notes
Because his fortress of solitude is facing foreclosure.
Instead of fighting against the opposition
He now goes toe to toe for
Promotions and positions;
And each time he gets 'em
It takes him a little bit further from who he wanted to be.
He's traded in his spandex for an AmEx and now
He gentrifies tall buildings in a single bound.
He's put all of his feelings in a lead safe
So even he can't make the mistake
Of seeing how he feels about the fellow he's become.
He's weak days because he spends his weekdays
And Krypton nights tasking beneath florescent lights
When his strength comes from basking in the yellow sun.
By the time he's 41 he will have forgotten he ever wanted to fly.
By 45 he'll have taken a position as a politician
And forgotten he never wanted to lie.
By 47 all thoughts of the Superman he wanted to become are almost gone.
He hasn't saved a life in years...
Not even his own.
And one night on the way home

He'll see some of his Justice League peers
Their S's emblazoned clear and true
They'll look at his suit cut, his beard
And they'll say, man, what happened to you?
And he'll say, I grew up!
And they'll say, yeah but
What did you grow into?
They'll say, look Clark we understand you've got to do what you got to do
You probably own property
Stocks, bonds and buildings
You probably live properly
And stand to make millions
But damn…
You used to want to be Superman.
You used to have plans to save Congolese women and South American children
Plans to fight against inequality, injustice, robber barons and corporate villains.
True you'd have probably never made a million
But you'd have certainly made a difference.

And I say to each of you Clark Kents reading this, I know
There is no phone booth that will allow you
To change back into your youth.
There is no closet to deposit this façade you've bought into
And re-emerge a god but you
Must try as hard as you might
To re-ignite the fire that has died
In your spirit, heart and eyes.
Forget the script and the lies.
Look into your mind

And find the Superman inside
Because Kent is a distraction and a disguise.
So leave yesterday's glasses and briefcase behind;
Tie your suit jacket around your neck.
Use the pen you use to sign your check
To write an "S" on your chest.
Now climb onto your desk
And point your hands toward the sky because you just may fly today.
The past is in the wind.
The present is here and gone again.
But the future... the future... is up, up... and away.

If You Should Ever Need It [Pt 3]

I have never forgotten;
It was the first day of kindergarten
And my mom was droppin' me off.
I thought I was clever I'd been plottin'.
To avoid it, I reported
That my chest felt tender and that I'd gotten a bad cough
That was killing me!
When really what the
Issue was
Was that what I was feeling was
Apprehension and tension toward
Starting at a new school;
But once my mom pulled out the castor oil and vapor rub
I told her, naw naw naw I'm good, I'm cool.
So as Monday morning would have it
We pulled in front of the building
In my mom's green Maverick
Around 9 or so
And she said, God bless the children,
Have a great day, here you go.
I sat there frozen staring at the car floor.
That's when my mom reached across my lap
Undid the lock and latch
And pushed open the car door.
She said she had
To be at work at 9
And it was already ten after;
She was already running ten minutes behind.
I was trying to find the nerve
But finally had to turn to her
On the verge of crying

And say … Momma, I'm scared.
She turned off the car right then and right there;
Laid my head in her lap
(Now eleven minutes late)
Rubbed my nervous back
Kissed my little face
And said Jonathan there is absolutely nothing wrong with that.
She said we all get frightened
Sometimes
That's just a part of life and
The most important thing in her eyes
Is how we handle the fear.
She said don't be afraid to be afraid
But also don't let the fear paralyze you dear.
I hugged her neck and dried my tears.
I made my way and joined my peers.
She was fifteen minutes late
As she drove away;
she waved, said she loved me
And that at the end of the day
For me she'd be on time.
She'd be waiting right here.

In my life she has always been right there;
Like when Angie broke my heart in High School.
I felt like dark clouds had begun to loom
There would never be another sunrise
The earth was clearly doomed
We'd certainly reached the end of times!
I was clearly consumed and half way out of my mind,
With heartache.
Then one day
Mom was in the kitchen

She'd just started to bake a cake.
I stood there in the doorway lookin' and listenin'.
I was just about to walk away
When she called for me to wait
And began to explain.
She said, baby I know
Mama's been through the same thing.
And I know fo' sho'
Your heart's going through some great pain
And right now puppy love
Must feel like a Great Dane
But this too shall pass.
You're going to look back on this too one day and laugh
But for now I need you to know
You're destined for some great things.
But in the meantime…
The chicken is almost done and the collards are off the chain!
I've got some cheesecake, some apple cake and little lemon meringue.
She said, by the time you're done with the meal
You're going to feel a little better;
And baby I know she looks cute in her boots, those tight jeans and
them sweaters
But a couple of years from now
You might mess around and forget you ever met her!
And we both laughed 'til we cried.

But some things you'll never forget no matter how hard you've tried.
I remember one night after the week daddy died;
Mama sat there humming a hymn.
She said, don't worry son everything's going to be all right.
She said, the strong are even strong when they're feeling weak inside
She said, your father's heart stopped
So it's yours that he's going to have to love, live and speak inside.

Now I'm a few years past thirty five,
And in my garden of good and evil when the clock strikes midnight
And my whole world is Evil Knievel and I just can't seem to get right
My phone just might ring.
And the part that's crazy
Is I'll pick it up and
My mom's on the other end
Saying, how you feeling baby?
I'll try to twist the plot
And ask her how her things are coming.
I'll tell her I'm okay
And she'll say
No you're not.
It's like she's psychic or something.
So I'll ask, Ma how'd you know?
And she'll say, boy you came from my womb you're connected to my
soul.
Then we'll talk on the phone for about an hour or so
Or until I feel better.
Then she'll say, before I let you go
There's one last thing I need to tell ya.
I'll always have a lap you can lay your troubles on,
An encouraging word
And a hymn to help you move your troubles along;
Some apple cake, some cheesecake and some loving arms
And I need you to believe it.
So son don't ever hesitate to call me
If you should ever need it.

CHAPTER SEVEN

"I miss you dearly"-Any child that has lost a parent, anywhere.

My Daddy's Hands

I've got my daddy's hands.
The back black and scotched,
Marked with the soot etched lines of dreams found and fulfilled;
Of hopes dropped and broken.
The creased and hilly topography reads like a Braille telling of my life,
of his life;
A travel guide to where he's been.
A road map to where I'm headed.

Hands that have held babies as bright and newly born
As the sun peeking, sneaking an eye just over the horizon
To spy if the day is ready to receive its warm gifts.

Hands that have held guns as old and dangerous
As ordering lunch at the counter during Jim Crow;
As actually having the money to pay the poll tax;
As "Blackie git from 'round here'n!"

Hands that have held lovers
As carefully, tenderly and lovingly
As a leaf nestling a dew drop deep into its curves, its crevices, its self.

Hands that have held bottles
As broken as homes in the wake of welfare;
As broken as a heart when a parent calls and says "The test came back.
Cancer, stage 4;"
As broken as the promise that you would never smoke or drink again.

Hands that have always, always been trying to hold their ground;
Hold back the doubts of others, of myself, of himself.
Hands pressed firmly against the immutable face of time

161

And watching the sand slip between our fingers as time's gaze grows
ever nearer.

Hands that fumble with the median, the mean, with partial measures.
Hands that don't know how to love you halfway, or trust you halfway
or want you halfway.
Hands that take definitive action.
Hands that either build pyramids or destroy paradigms
But let you know where they stand.

My Daddy's hands!
Aged by picket signs and bar room brawls.
Aged in store front churches and back alley dice games.
Aged from being underpaid and overlooked.

They shake like they are at a fault line or at fault and lyin'
But in truth they tremble with anger, rancor and frustration
Born through the generations.

In my palm I hold the pennies paid sharecroppers.
Beneath his nails you will find the skin from an overseer's face.
Our knuckles are bruised and broken from beating against walls of
oppression;
That is when they aren't bent and intertwined in supplication and
reverence
Knuckles pressed into piety and prayer
As white as the God I was told made us in his reflection;
As white as the Jesus we were told was always ours.

I used to hide my hands, hard, aged, damaged and shaking
But I've learned to take them from my pockets;
To pull them from behind my back, to present them proudly to the
world;

And when people stare and inquire about my hands provenance
I take their hands into mine and say "I've got my daddy's hands…
what did your father give you?"

ACKNOWLEDGEMENTS

First and foremost I must acknowledge God (but not in that corny, I just won a Grammy for putting out an album that debases the world kind of way). Some of my earliest memories are of the church, are of Martin Luther King Jr. fans and holding sweaty hands in hot sanctuaries as we all bowed our heads to acknowledge something greater than ourselves. On days when I didn't think I'd live to see the night and nights when I cried until it was a new day I always had the prayers taught to me by my mother and great grandmother on my mind, heart and lips. Without my faith and belief in God I cannot imagine where I'd be, what I'd be doing or even who I'd be.

Barbara Goode: They say that the word for God on the lips of a child is mother. They sometimes get it right.

John Goode Jr.: Not a day passes when you are not in my thoughts.

Tiffany Goode: If a person is fortunate enough to in this lifetime get a best friend that is also their sibling they are doubly blessed and fortunate indeed. I am doubly blessed and fortunate indeed.

Duane, Leisa, Cheryl and Yvette Goode: What you have meant to me over the years as my brothers and sisters is immeasurable and indescribable. As a child I looked up to you all. As an adult, though taller than all of you, I still look up.

Joshua Goode: My man! When I think of the bright future. When I think of all that is good in the world. When I think of progress. When I think of intelligence. When I think of endless possibility. When I think of … hope. I think of you. Few things honor me more than being your Uncle.

164

Gunther Gordon: There is the family you're born with and the family that you over time create. You sir are my brother from another mother of that there is no question, debate or doubt.

Keda (aka Mira) what you've meant to me over the years is without question. Bonnie we don't talk as much as we should but know that you are always in my thoughts. Spinxx, man if I wasn't me I'd be you! Amir, you always know that my home and ear are available to you. In the future we will co-create content that will change the world. Malik you will always be my brother. Cola Rum whenever I need an honest, unfiltered word I dial your number. Tammy you are the reason I found my way to Georgia and I don't know if I'd have found my voice anywhere else. Rhee-Diddy let's make up a story using song titles. Dana what haven't we told each other? Renita we've been in each others corner since Bunamore. Mr. Shelton thanks for all the kind words and support over the years. Dr. Bascomb you have been a Godsend! Jamika when times were most dark you brought a light. Thank you for all of your help in editing this book. Southside RVA (Oak Grove, Bellemeade, Blackwell) thanks for helping to shape me. Atlanta, GA thanks for finding the artist in me.